Jim Britt's

Cracking the Rich Code[14]

Inspiring Stories, Insights and Strategies from Top Thought Leaders Around the World

STAY IN TOUCH WITH JIM BRITT

www.JimBritt.com

www.CrackingTheRichCode.com

www.PowerOfLettingGo.com

Cracking the Rich Code[14]

Jim Britt

All Rights Reserved

Copyright 2024

CTRC Publishing and Training, Inc.

10556 Combie Road, Suite 6205

Auburn, CA 95602

The use of any part of this publication, whether reproduced, stored in any retrieval system, or transmitted in any forms or by any means, electronic or otherwise, without the prior written consent of the publisher, is an infringement of copyright law.

Jim Britt

Cracking the Rich Code[14]

ISBN:

Co-authors from Around the World

Jim Britt

Tanya Steele

Andrew Hurst

Eric Lopkin

Jennifer Jehl

Sue Bodine

Lucie Leduc

Manny Lopez

Mike Oglesbee

Onyx Jones

Luz Maria Villanueva

Michael Jacobs

Dr. Jason I. Henderson

Jennifer Brown

Tammy Vallieres

Sallyann Angerami Martinez

Diane L. Smyers

Dr. Ken Rochon

Yolanda Martinez

Nathalie Plamondon-Thomas

Jane Williams

Dr. Mindy Gewirtz

DEDICATION

Entrepreneurs will change the world. They always have and they always will.

Dedicated to the entrepreneurial spirit that lives within each of us. God Bless America and the World!

PREFACE

Jim Britt

The world's top 50 most influential speakers and top 20 life and success strategist.

In pursuit of a meaningful and fulfilling life, the concept of richness extends far beyond mere financial prosperity. It encompasses a holistic approach, embracing abundance in every facet of our existence—financial, emotional, intellectual, and spiritual. "Cracking the Rich Code with 21 Top Thought Leaders" is not just a manual for accumulating wealth; it is a comprehensive guide to attaining riches in all areas of life.

The journey to holistic riches is a transformative odyssey, and within these pages, you'll find the collective wisdom of 21 experts who have not only achieved remarkable success in their respective field but, have also cracked the code to living a truly rich and fulfilling life, while helping other to do the same. Their stories, insights, and strategies are the keys to unlocking doors to prosperity abundance and well-being.

Our esteemed contributors are visionaries who understand that true richness transcends financial accomplishments. Their perspectives span the spectrum, from business, to personal development, mindfulness, relationships, health and wellness, and spirituality. Each chapter in this book serves as a beacon of guidance, offering a unique perspective on how to navigate the intricate pathways of life to attain richness in all dimensions.

As you delve into the following pages, you'll be introduced to the stories of these remarkable individuals who have not only achieved success in their respective fields, but have also cultivated richness in their relationships, health, and sense of purpose. Their experiences are a testament to the idea that true wealth is a compellation of material prosperity and the riches found in our connections, personal growth, and the alignment of our actions with our deepest values.

True richness moves beyond the material realm into emotional richness. Emotional intelligence, resilience, and the ability to navigate the complexities of human relationships. Each coauthor offers practical tools and perspectives that will empower you to forge deeper connections, overcome challenges, and find joy in your everyday interactions.

Intellectual richness is also a dimension often overlooked in the pursuit of a rich life. From innovation and creativity to conscious learning and adaptability, intellectual richness is the fuel that propels us forward. All creation begins with an idea. The contributors share their insights into cultivating a curious mind, staying ahead of a rapidly changing world, and leveraging knowledge to create a life of richness and purpose.

Spiritual richness takes center stage too. Beyond religious affiliations, spiritual richness encompasses a profound connection with oneself, others, and the universe. These thought leaders share their journeys of self-discovery, mindfulness, and the pursuit of a higher purpose, offering a more rich and meaningful existence.

This book is not a one-size-fits-all prescription for richness; it a diverse tapestry of ideas, experiences, and strategies that you can tailor to your unique journey. Whether you are an entrepreneur seeking business and financial success, or an individual navigating the complexities of relationships. A lifelong learner, or someone on a spiritual quest, "Cracking the Rich Code" has something for you.

As you embark on this transformative journey with our diverse lineup of thought leaders and experts, just remember that richness is not a destination but a continuous exploration. May the insights and strategies within these pages serve as catalysts for your personal and collective growth, guiding you toward a life of richness in every sense of the word.

Wishing you abundance fulfillment, and richness in all areas of your life.

And remember, just one idea acted upon can change your life. Happy hunting!

Jim Britt

www.JimBritt.com

www.CrackingTheRichCode.com

www.PowerOfLettingGo.com

Foreword by Brian Tracy

Life is always a series of transitions... people, places and things that shape who we are as individuals. Often, you never know that the next catalyst for change is just around the corner, in someone you meet, on a page of a book or in a moment of self-reflection.

As the author of 93 books myself, you can imagine how fussy I am to write a foreword to publications in the business and self-development space. My friend Jim Britt is an exception. He has spent decades influencing millions of individuals with his many best-selling books, seminars, programs and coaching, to blossom into the best version of themselves. He has the knowledge, wisdom and skillsets needed to make a significant contribution to overcoming issues entrepreneurs face in business today. His success speaks for itself.

In a world where the pursuit of wealth and success often dominates our collective consciousness, the concept of cracking the rich code has become an elusive quest for many. We marvel at the seemingly effortless success stories of millionaires and billionaires, wondering what secret knowledge or hidden talents they possess that have propelled them to riches. Yet, behind every success story lies a unique and inspiring journey, woven with challenges, triumphs, and invaluable lessons learned.

It is with great excitement that I present to you "Cracking the Rich Code," a book that unveils the remarkable successes of 20 millionaire coauthors. These individuals have not only achieved extraordinary success, but have also generously shared their insights, strategies, and wisdom, inviting the readers to embark on their own transformative journeys.

Within these pages you will discover a variety of stories that defy the myth of an easily attainable overnight success. Instead, you will discover stories of resilience, determination and the unrelenting decisions to pursue their dreams. Each author offers a unique perspective on wealth creation, sharing the secrets they unlocked along their path to financial success.

As you read each chapter you will encounter diverse backgrounds, highlighting the fact that the rich code is not for a certain gender, race, age or social status. You will discover that there are a myriad of ways in which financial success can be achieved.

So, prepare to be inspired as you witness the transformative power of perseverance and the unwavering belief in one's abilities. Through their stories, each coauthor will take you behind the scenes of their successes, allowing you a glimpse into the countless hours of hard work, sacrifices, and failures they encountered along the way.

This book is not just about destination; it's about the journey. Beyond the accumulation of wealth, these authors emphasize the importance of personal growth, finding purpose, and making a positive impact on the world. They share their experience of self-discovery and self-improvement, and offer guidance on developing the mindset, habits, and values necessary to build sustainable success in any and all areas of life.

Their stories will reveal that the rich code is not a hidden secret, but rather a blueprint for anyone willing to embrace the principles with dedication and perseverance. It's about learning from failures, embracing risks, overcoming fears, and continuously expanding one's knowledge and skills. It's about having a mindset of abundance, nurturing relationships, and giving back to society.

Whether you are an aspiring entrepreneur, a seasoned professional, or simply seeking inspiration and guidance, "Cracking the Rich Code" will provide a roadmap to unlocking your real potential. Through the diverse perspectives of Jim Britt and the coauthors, you will find a wealth of actionable strategies, that will empower you to rewrite your own story and chart your course toward financial prosperity.

Let's help in this quest, as Jim Britt and the talented coauthors unselfishly donate their most important asset, their precious LIFETIME of experience, to elevate one life at a time to their full potential and greatness.

If I were you, I would buy 10, and then giftwrap them to acknowledge your most important top ten relationships in life or clients in business. By doing so, you will strengthen the relationship and encourage others to live a more fulfilling life.

As you close the pages of any of the books in this series, you will gain a new life of clarity and focus as never before. *Cracking the Rich Code* will provide tools to transform results for corporations, institutions, and individuals, both personally and financially.

If you've ever wanted to read a book that challenges you to become more than you are and leaves you with enough inspiration to last a lifetime, *Cracking the Rich Code* is it!

Allow all you have read in this book to create introspection and redirection if required.

Remember, death is certain. Success is not. This life is your journey to craft.

Brian Tracy

Table of Content

PREFACE vii
Foreword by Brian Tracy xi
Jim Britt 1
    Reinvent Your Money Philosophy
Sue Bodine 19
    How To Be Your Own Financial Architect: Building Generational Wealth
Tammy Vallieres and Sylvia Tam 31
    Raising Empowered Kids with Hero Intelligence: Our Mission & Methodology
Sallyann A. Martinez 45
    The Empowerment of Finding Yourself…A Letter to Myself
Yolanda Martinez 55
    The Foundation of Female Empowerment
Dr. Jason I. Henderson 67
    Understanding the 5 levels of Wealth Creation.
Ken 'Dr. Smiley' Rochon, Jr., PhD 77
    The Evolution of Dr. Smiley
Manny Lopez 87
    "Dear Me"
Jennifer Jehl 95
    Run to Your Self
Lucie Leduc 107
    Leading with Curiosity: A Story of Growth and Adaptation
Jane Williams 119

Rethinking Entrepreneurship: Can a Corporation be the Way to Find Your Fire?

Michael Jacobs **129**

My Journey as an Entrepreneur: Wisdom Gained from Lessons Learned

Onyx Jones **139**

31 Days to Prosperity

Nathalie Plamondon-Thomas, CSP® **149**

Finances: The No.1 Cause of Stress: Think Yourself® Wealthy

Mike Oglesbee **159**

From Surrender to Success: Harnessing My Hidden Potential

Luz Maria Villanueva, MA., Ph.D., ... **169**

Passion and Grit: An Entrepreneur's Journey through Light and Darkness. How I Reinvented Myself, Rediscovered My Passion, and Transformed from Employee to Entrepreneur

Eric Lopkin **181**

Success Starts with Taking Care of People

Andrew Hurst **191**

The Coaching Process

Jennifer Brown **201**

From Stuck to Soaring: Unleash Your Potential

Tanya Steele **213**

Rivers of Service: A Journey of True Wealth

Diane Smyers **223**

Unconditional Love : Compassion Interrupted

Dr. Mindy Gewirtz **233**

7 Leadership Secrets for Living a Life That Works:The Adaptive Framework

Afterword **245**

Jim Britt

Jim Britt is an award-winning author of 15 best-selling books and ten #1 International best-sellers. Some of his many titles include Rings of Truth, Do This. Get Rich- For Entrepreneurs, Unleashing Your Authentic Power, The Power of Letting Go, Cracking the Rich Code and The Entrepreneur.

Jim is an internationally recognized business and life strategist who is highly sought after as a keynote speaker, both online and live, for all audiences.

As an entrepreneur Jim has launched 28 successful business ventures. He has served as a success strategist to over 300 corporations worldwide and is one of the world's top 50 most influential speakers and top 20 life and business success strategists. He was presented with the "Best of the Best" award out of the top 100 contributors of all time to the Direct Selling industry.

For over four decades Jim has presented seminars throughout the world sharing his success strategies and life enhancing realizations with over 5,000 audiences, totaling almost 2,000,000 people from all walks of life.

Early in his speaking career he was in business with the late Jim Rohn for eight years, where Tony Robbins worked under Jim's direction for his first few years in the speaking business.

As a performance strategist, Jim leverages his skills and experience as one of the leading experts in peak performance, entrepreneurship and personal empowerment to produce stellar results. He is pleased to work with small business entrepreneurs, and anyone seeking to remove the blocks that stop their success in any area of their life.

One of Jim's latest programs "Cracking the Rich Code" focuses on the subconscious programs influencing one's relationship with money and their financial success.www.CrackingTheRichCode.com

Reinvent Your Money Philosophy

By Jim Britt

Once again that uncomfortable feeling pays a visit, but this time you can't close the door and just ignore it. The discomfort that you are feeling is with yourself. You feel like your life does not fit you anymore. Maybe it hasn't for a long time. But do you dare reinvent yourself and your money philosophy? Do you have the courage to take the necessary steps to let go of the person you are today, and used to be, so that you can blossom into the person you have always wanted to become financially? This can sometimes feel scary because you have to let go of attachments you have to money in order to reinvent your new money philosophy. If you are up to reinventing yourself and ready to travel along a new path to where you have never been, now is the perfect time to get started, and I want to help.

The process of reinventing yourself is very empowering. In fact, you can apply this philosophy to any area of your life. If you want something more in any area of life you have to reinvent yourself into someone different than you are today. But let's start with reinventing your money philosophy.

You might not realize it yet, but you do have all it takes to truly ignite change financially.

Don't let anybody else tell you otherwise. The first thing you will need to do is take a look at yourself. What do you want to change about yourself? Because all change starts inside you.

Since you are starting over so to speak, if you are going to dream, might as well dream big. Think of yourself as an author who is writing your new life story, your new money philosophy. You are limited only by your imagination. Before you start reinventing yourself, you have to at least know what you're working with and what you want changed. The more specific you are, the better. This will give you direction and allow you to focus on the right things.

If you ask someone what the most important thing in their life is, most often they will answer "family" or "their health." But is that actually true? Because, when you look at where the average person spends most of their waking hours, it is focused on making money. So, money must be the most important area for most…at least until they have all they want to feel financially secure. Again, since you are reinventing yourself and your money philosophy, if you are going to dream, you might as well dream big.

So, what's the secret to incredible financial success? The secret is, there is no <u>one</u> secret! The reality is there are many "secrets" that work together in combination with one another, giving you the winning "combination" to succeed financially! Think of financial success like a giant vault at the bank with a thick steel door blocking it and a combination lock. Unless you have the right combination to that lock, it doesn't matter how much you beat on the door, how hard you work, how many lists you make, or good intentions you have. Because there is a combination you must know to unlock that door and get it to swing open so you can walk through to the other side where the money is.

Many years ago, I met a very wealthy person, and I asked what inspired him to be wealthy? His answer really surprised me. He said, "Money is a game and the person with the most notches on his belt wins." I was shocked! I was a young man at the time and having grown up without much I wanted to become wealthy. Yet after hearing this person's response, I looked deeper into his eyes and frankly, he didn't seem all that happy, and the sense of lack of balance in his life was apparent. He was out of shape and had a look in his eyes of anxiety, loneliness and anger. I could tell that he had stepped on a lot of people to get to where he was. I knew right then I didn't want to take his approach.

How about you? Do you think that being financially wealthy takes putting yourself first and trampling over those that get in your way? Hopefully not. Do you think that being wealthy means putting the lust for money ahead of everything else? I sure hope not. On the other hand, I've met very wealthy people who give back to their community, have large circles of friends, and always seemed to be happy and abundant in so many other ways. In fact, a couple years ago I took a camera crew around the country and interviewed twelve self-made mega millionaires and one billionaire. The requirement was that they all had to have started with nothing. In other words, they didn't inherit their wealth. And all twelve made their money in different industries...

Internet marketing, network marketing, traditional business, real estate, television, direct sales, social media, etc. If you asked any of these twelve individuals the same question, you'd likely get this sort of answer: "Wealth is simply a vehicle that magnify your deeper personality traits and mindset."

The following is what I have learned from my own experiences and the experiences of these twelve mega-millionaires and others I have associated myself with over the years. Wealth is the ultimate power of leverage. It gives you options as to how you want to live. Nothing is truer about becoming wealthy than this. It is a magnifying glass into your money mindset and philosophy.

Wouldn't it be nice if you could simply decide to become wealthy and you did? Well, let me fill you in on a big secret...you can! You already know the basics. You know that you should pay off your debt and start budgeting. You know that all you need to do is regularly invest money in your savings and other investments and let time do the work. Spend less, save more, build your investment portfolio...you've heard it time and time again. Then why aren't you on the way to becoming wealthy? Maybe you are. If so, congratulations. There are many reasons that people don't take action, even though they have the information. The reality is that so many people are just simply afraid to change. Fear takes a lot away from a person. They don't want to fail but when you buy into fear it will take you down that path.

Here's one key to the vault's combination lock. For things to change for you financially, you have to make a change, otherwise you'll continue to keep producing the same results you've been producing. This may come as a shock to you, but most people really don't want to change.

Just give them a beer, point them toward the sofa and give them the television remote and a bag of chips. They will continue to complacently live out their lives, while complaining about what they don't have, and criticizing others for what they have. Their wealth philosophy is to earn a living and get by. They spend the majority of their time focused on what they *don't have* and what they *don't want*, on how to pay the bills, instead of focusing on what they *do have* and what they *do want* in their lives. Nothing wrong with this philosophy if that is what you want. But if it is not what you want, then *everything* is wrong with that philosophy.

I know people, as I'm sure you do, that love having the drama of being up to their ears in debt.

It's a balance beam that keeps excitement in their lives. It's a roller coaster ride that is thrilling, but always drops them off at the same place time and time again. But at such a huge cost! What they don't realize is that they can't maintain their balance or thrill forever. At some point you have to decide where to get off… or you simply fall off!

Most have been conditioned to believe that creating wealth is difficult, or that it's only for the lucky few. They convince themselves that "someday" they are going to be a success, to start their own business, to make a financial plan for their future, to have all they want in life…someday. Someday…what an interesting concept. Think of all the things that were supposed to have happened by now…that someday that you may have convinced yourself was just around the corner. To most, that someday is where they have convinced themselves they would be right now, if only they had more time, more talent, more education, more money, or maybe a better opportunity available. One of the things I discovered is that wealthy people think differently. They don't wait until someday. They decide and execute. They do things that the majority of people are not willing to do.

Before going any further, I would urge you to stop right now and take a realistic look at your last five years. Have you truly made progress? Are the last five years what *you* wanted? Are you where you thought you would be today financially? And, most importantly, do you have a solid plan for the next five?

Too many people like to complain, but just don't want to make the effort. They don't have time. They'll do it next year. Let me tell you, you have to find time to get your financial situation in order if you want to gain wealth…and freedom…ever! Time is costing you money. The more time you spend trying to pay off credit cards, the more you pay the credit card companies and contribute to their wealth. I'm not saying to ignore your financial obligations. What I'm saying is that paying off your credit cards, although a good place to start, will not bring you wealth. Why? Because after you pay them off you are still left with the mentality that charged them to the max in the first place. You *can* have all the money you want. It just takes learning and developing the traits that rich people use, and some time to make it happen. If you want to change your financial situation you have to reinvent yourself, because the old you won't cut it. To become wealthy, you will need to develop some vital traits.

Let me offer you the number sequence to the vault. First is a *firm decision* to become wealthy. Wealthy people you will find make solid decisions and commit to seeing them through. And decisions always come before the answers. Those who are *not* financially successful put off decisions or mess around with their decision once it is made… and have a lot of excuses why things are not working. That is the language of the poor. Mediocrity cannot be an option if you want to attain wealth. And wealth is whatever you say it is. A decision to be wealthy creates a wealthy mindset, and your mindset determines how you show up in the world. I'm not talking about deciding *how* to earn the money. Again, the decision comes first, then the how to.

It is really surprising though; how many people fear making that decision. They do all sorts of things to keep the moment of decision at arms-length including:

Gathering more data.

Getting ready to get going…

As soon as this or that happens, I'll get going…

I need to do more research…

I need to get some other's opinion…

Fretting over who the decision might offend.

Worrying about the resources needed to pull off the decision.

Or hoping they will just get lucky and make the money they need without making a decision, etc.

The real problem is that most are stuck in a comfort zone and making a decision would mean having to do something different, that might be a bit painful. I suppose that is a decision we all face…the pain of staying stuck in our current situation or the pain of change. Most people would rather live with the "old you" for fear that becoming the "new you" would be too painful.

If that is you, then you can close the book now, and get back to the TV and potato chips. If you are not willing to make a decision to change no one can help you.

Let's say you make a decision to be wealthy. Whatever wealth means to you. What happens next when the old programs, the old habit patterns and mind chatter kicks in?

"Wait a minute! What makes you think you have the talent to become wealthy?"

"I've never done it before! Maybe I really can't become wealthy."

"Besides, I don't have the expertise, time, money, etc., to become wealthy."

And before long all the self-talk has changed your decision into something totally different from becoming wealthy. Wealth is a mindset.

I remember a friend of mine had created a hair care line that actually grew hair. He planned to sell it by placing it into drugstore chains. He had the connections to get it into the stores across the country. However, after months the line just wasn't selling. Instead of just giving up, a business associate told him about a new marketing concept, a TV infomercial. This was one of the first, if not the first, TV infomercial ever produced. So, nobody knew if it would actually work.

My friend was a decision maker, so he said let's do it. That decision turned into over $200 million in sales that netted him almost $100 million. The point is, he could have given up on his first attempt. Again, wealth is a mindset.

One of the mega millionaires I interviewed went bankrupt three times and today has a net worth of over $500 million. My point is that you don't give up just because one approach to becoming wealthy doesn't work. There are thousands of ways to become wealthy, but without a wealth mindset nothing—ever---happens.

Remember this: <u>Every income level requires a different you</u>. You have to reinvent yourself, your mindset, your money philosophy, for each new income level. You have to be willing to let go of the *old you* and embrace the challenge of becoming the *new you*.

If you want to learn, grow and change, you have to hang around people that challenge you to become better. If you want to become a million dollar a year earner, but yet you hang around and take input from people earning $60,000 a year, you'll likely to be right where they are financially. I'm not putting them down. I'm just saying that those you hang around most are what you'll become.

I know people, as I'm sure you do, who go to work every day to a job that they hate. They hate what they earn and/or what they do, but they stay because they feel they have no other choice. They justify their position by calling it job security. But what they don't realize is that there is no security in a job! Unless you are a smart investor, it's called *prolonged poverty* in my book! It's like living in a place you hate but you're afraid to move because of your job. Then you lose your job and can't afford to move, so you look for another insecure position that will keep you in the place you hate. *That's a sort of insanity, don't you think?*

What would I say to a person in that position? "If you want to get better, you have to make better decisions, and you have to hang out with and take input from those who've done what you want to do." I would say "if you want to be rich, you have to stop working for someone else's goals and dreams and make a decision to start working for your own." If you want to become wealthy, you have to stop with the employee mentality, reinvent yourself, and start thinking like wealthy people think."

The first step is to make the decision, one that doesn't allow for anything less. Up until the decision is made nothing happens...except, of course, the decision to stay where you are now. In reality not making a decision is a decision to leave everything status quo.

The next trait all wealthy people have in common is that they are *bold*. Financially successful people have learned that action is vital. And often times that requires a level of boldness. They know that procrastination kills. They live with the reality of consequences and know there will always be uncertainty in decisions, but they boldly step forward and make the decision anyway.

Just like my friend with the hair care product. No one can see all possible ramifications; no one can predict every contingency; no one can absolutely prevent failure...or assure success. However, the wealth minded person knows that failure is not final. It's just one of those possible outcomes that happens on their way to success.

The real danger surrounding decision making is not, *"Will I make the wrong decision, but did I make the best decision possible given the facts and circumstances."* Success minded individuals invest in learning what they need to make the correct decisions from those who have done what they want to do. But, when it comes to investing in mentorship, so often I hear people say, "I can't afford it." "It costs too much." When in reality they can't afford not to." And without mentorship, it costs...way... too much!

I remember the time when my home was in foreclosure, both my vehicles and all my furniture had been repossessed ...and I had less than a dollar to my name. Then, someone, a mentor, sat with me for two hours, helped me to get my head on straight, taught me a few things, and eliminated some mistakes, and my business took off like a rocket... to the tune of a million dollars in the next 12 month. That was back when a million was really a million.

The real question is, *"What do you really want?"* Are you just dreaming about success and wealth or standing on the sidelines observing other people's successes and wishing you had what they have? Do you justify why you are not financially successful? Or are you bold enough to take responsibility, step out into the spotlight and take center stage before you have all the answers?

Do you really want to be rich? And if so, what would financial success look like to you? Most people have never defined what financial success would be for them, and that's why they've never made a decision and taken bold action to have it. And that is the only reason they don't have it!

The two most important question that you can ask yourself is, "Have I defined what financial success means to me?" And two, "Am I basing my future financial success on past experiences or on what I really want?" How you answer those questions can change your life!

Often times there is a feature in the investment section of some of the entrepreneurial magazines. It's a success story column about people who've made it big financially. You'll find stories of individuals who have carved out a niche for themselves in selected fields, lived a fulfilled life serving others with their skills and amassed quite a fortune while doing so. You will always find one common trait in all the featured personalities. Not in one of them. Not some of them. But this trait is in all of them! It is called a "wealth mindset." Despite the fact that they're from different backgrounds, all of them possess the same philosophy when it comes to money. Wealthy people think differently. This is the infamous *"money consciousness"* that most of the motivational and personal development trainers speak of so often in their books and seminars.

This wealth philosophy basically means this: Regardless of the physical condition that you may be currently in, as long as you see yourself bathing in financial abundance, your actions will maneuver, and circumstances will unfold in a way to create the wealth that you see yourself enjoying.

If you possess that wealth mindset, you will have the Midas touch when it comes to earning money. If you don't, you won't. That simple. The fortunate thing is all of us possess the innate ability to fire up this wealth mindset.

The key is letting go of the old you and reinventing the new you that you want to become.

First is making the *decision* to be wealthy. Second is being *bold*. Next, is *letting go* of your limiting beliefs about money and changing how you relate to money.

Some people frown at the mere mention of money. How many times have you heard people say something like this: "Oh, I'm not doing this for the money" or "Money isn't everything." Well, they're not wrong. Money isn't everything. The fact is that money in itself has no value. It is the things that money can buy when in circulation that make it so valuable. Money can buy material possessions for sure. But personal freedom is what we all seek, and we all deserve to have what we want.

Money gives you options. Those who say that money doesn't matter, I can guess with 100% accuracy that they are most likely broke! How could they not be if "money doesn't matter" is their focus? At the same time, if you look from a different angle, once you've got enough money to be financially free, it can literally change what you do from laborious work to spending more precious moments with your family and friends as well as doing the things you love. In essence, if you never come to terms with what money can bring forth into your life, its real value, your uneasiness with the "idea" of money, it will limit your ability to create more of it.

To put it simply, just imagine this: would you go into a car showroom if you've never had the intention to purchase a car? You may not want to buy it now, but the fact that you walked into the showroom implies that you appreciate the value of what a car brings. It can serve as a means of transportation for you and your family. And because of the perceived value you see in owning a car, you'll find the means and ways to get one. Having money is the same. Once you see its value, believe you can have it, and want it like it is as essential as owning a car, you'll find the ways and means to getting it. Heck. Even those that are broke and spend their last few dollars on lottery tickets see the value of money. Remember, you can't create something that you're not in harmony with or that you haven't decided to have. Therefore, it becomes imperative that before you move onto other steps to really "get" this wealth mindset concept, you should definitely have a conversation with yourself, or someone that can mentor you, to let go of the beliefs, if you have them, that's limiting you about money.

Having money means…finish the sentence…

What came up? Do you feel your answer will move you toward being wealthy?

Answer these questions:

Why do you deserve to be wealthy?

What do you believe about money?

How did you come to believe this?

Who taught you to believe that way?

Were they wealthy?

Who taught them?

Is my money mindset based on past experiences or beliefs?

The only way to change a limiting belief is to challenge it. A belief is something that you have decided is true…it may not be at all. A belief is simply a decision that something is true…and it may have been made by someone else and passed down to you. The good news is that you can change your belief simply by changing your decisions and letting go of your old programming. If you want to be wealthy, you must first decide to be wealthy…whatever being wealthy means to you.

The next combination to the vault is to decide *"why"* you want to be wealthy. What is the payoff for wealth? Why you want something is the fuel, the passion, that will take you where you want to go. It fuels the passion behind the decision.

Everyone has the right to be wealthy. You have the right to be wealthy….and yet, most allow a temporary lack of money to eat into their minds, literally confining them into a vicious cycle of mediocrity. The bottom line is that people are not wealthy because they have not yet decided to be wealthy. So long as you make a conscious decision to become wealthy and have utmost faith that you can achieve it, and you let go of your outdated beliefs about money, you will act accordingly to what you believe. So, why not say "yes" to getting wealthy today! And say it with conviction.

Deciding to be wealthy only gets you started on the quest, but what sustains you throughout the journey is the *"why"* you want to be wealthy, and letting go of the mind chatter that pulls you back into your old habit patterns.

What is the real reason that you want an extra $1 million in your bank account, or you want to earn a million dollars a year? Again, wealth is whatever you say it is. Could be $10,000 a month coming in from investments. What I know for sure is that, if you do not have a burning desire supporting your decision, and you don't let go of your old way of thinking and believing, you'll find your inspiration tapering off sooner and your decision fading into something totally different to being wealthy. That is the trap that most everyone falls into.

Try this exercise. Take a piece of paper and scribble down all the reasons that you can think of why you want to be wealthy. Maybe you would like to retire earlier and travel around the world? Or maybe you want to quit your job and be a full-time parent? Write down as many reasons as you can think of. Needless to say, the one that resonates with the deepest part of your heart should be written on an index card to remind you of the outcome you desire. Paste it to your forehead!

Again, wealth can be whatever you say it is. For some it might mean ten million in the bank. For others it might mean having enough residual income coming monthly to completely cover their overhead. For example, if it's $5,000 per month that you're looking for, working in your existing job and going for a raise in pay might suffice. However, if $100,000 per month is what you intend to achieve, other alternatives such as starting your own business, investing in properties or working on your skills sets to better serve the marketplace will probably be more effective.

More importantly, knowing how much you want prepares your mind for the potential issues you may face to make that happen. The more you want, the more challenges you face to get it. The challenge therefore becomes: how do you know how much you want? Arbitrarily quoting a figure will probably do you more harm than good. If the amount you pull out of the sky is much higher than what you really want, your approach to acquire wealth may not be in harmony with why you want it and you may end up burning yourself out. In the event that the amount is lesser than what you really want, then you'll find yourself re-adjusting why you want it, which may not inspire you to keep going. Your "what" your "why" and your "decision" and "mindset" need to be in harmony. How you get there is not important at this moment.

Suppose you want to get from point "A" to point "B." There's route 1, route 2, 3 all the way to infinity. When you believe that there is only one way to get there, it limits your possibilities. When you are totally open to how to get there, the mind starts considering the many options and may prompt you to act on one of them that you haven't even thought of before. Along the way, your wealthy mindset may allow you to recognize different opportunities, encouraging you to change course and go through a totally different experience than originally planned.

I remember steve who attained wealth in a totally different manner than expected. Initially, his plan was to market his own music compositions through conventional methods. But he instead stumbled upon online internet marketing and embarked on an unconventional route to becoming an internet millionaire. It was not an easy route, because he had to juggle learning about the new internet marketing model of which he knew nothing about while still working a full-time job. But his burning desire to be rich got him through the hurdle and eventually to financial freedom.

Start to imagine yourself as already having wealth. Before you physically acquire the wealth that you have envisioned, you need to own it as if you already possess the amount of money that you desire! In other words, how would you feel right now if you were wealthy? What would you be doing differently? How would your life be different? How would your day unfold?

Start to "own" the result of your wealth now! Here's why. The subconscious mind is unable to differentiate between actual possession and mere visualization. So, by imagining that you already have it, you are encouraging your subconscious mind to seek ways to transform your imaginary feelings into the real thing. I know many people refute this type of thinking as impractical. But if you think about it, isn't everything around us a true manifestation of someone else's imagination? Everything manmade was in someone's imagination before it was created. And when they possessed the passion to create it, the ways and means appeared. The wright brothers imagined being able to fly, and the reality is, we are now able to fly in an airplane from one country to another in a matter of hours. And it didn't happen with their first trial.

I recently flew on an 880 Air Bus from San Francisco to Dubai. It holds 700 passengers, and the wingspan is 30 feet shy of the length of a football field. I'll bet with Wright brothers would be impressed.

Thomas Edison imagined lighting a whole room using a single source, and as a result, the light bulb was invented! Yes, it took a few tries, about 10,000, but eventually he created it, and now it lights the world.

Look around right now. If you are in a room, look at all the things in that room that made someone wealthy. Why not you? Take a walk outside and look around. How many things do you see that made someone wealthy? Why not you? It all started in someone's imagination. They owned it first in their mind and heart before it became a reality. It's a fact that without the imagination of great visionaries, we would not be able to enjoy many things that we enjoy today. Refrigerators, radio, television, automobiles, cell phones and thousands of other great inventions we would not enjoy today if not for someone first imagining it into existence.

You too possess the same capability to create and improve your own destiny by constructing it in your mind first. The decision comes first, then the answers! All improvement in your life begins in the improvement of your mental pictures. Change your mental pictures and you change the outcome of your life, like changing a channel on TV.

For example, you can imagine receiving income checks when you open the mailbox every day. Or you can picture yourself receiving an award for being nominated the best entrepreneur in your country or having a #1 best-selling book. Not only does it send the message to your subconscious, but it also serves as a great form of daily inspiration.

It is absolutely essential to have a crystal-clear picture of what you want to accomplish before you begin. If you want to attain wealth you must learn to operate with a sharply defined mental image of the outcome you want to attain. Focus your attention on the spot where you want to land, not on where you are now, or on any misconceptions or shortcomings you may think you have. In other words, visualize your arrival and you will develop a magnetic harmony with the ways and means required to get there. Solutions will begin to appear, and obstacles will seem to disappear. Answers will come to you. People will show up to support you in your endeavor.

Look at the end result as something that you are already prepared to do, you just haven't done it yet.

Think about this. Your success is something that you have been preventing, it is not something you have to struggle to make happen.

You'll find the solutions taking you toward your goals will come to you in the most unexpected and sudden ways when you let go of the old you, reinvent a new you, and embrace your new money philosophy. You don't need the *perfect* plan first. What you need is a *perfectly* clear decision about your success, which creates the right mindset, and the ideal way to get there will materialize.

You can't get all the answers up front so don't waste your time trying. The success formula doesn't involve getting everything neatly organized, with everything in its proper place and sequence and all the risks eliminated before you make the move. If you want that, then get a 9-5 job, but realize that will never make you wealthy. Get a target…point, then take action! Your true greatness lies within your ability to decide what you want and commitment to having it, and then taking bold action to get it.

The world you have visualized in the past is the world you now live in. The world you visualize now is the world you will create in the future. And the world you create is limited only by your imagination, your mindset, and your ability to let go of the old beliefs that keep you stuck and to reinvent the new you.

Everyone has the right to be wealthy. You have the right to be wealthy. Yet, most allow a temporary lack of money to eat into their minds, literally confining them into the vicious cycle of mediocrity. The bottom line is that people are poor because they have not yet decided to be rich.

We create our own reality either unconsciously without purpose or consciously with a purpose. A person who believes that the universe is abundant, and they can attain whatever level of financial success they desire…and a person who believes that money only comes from working hard and will receive money only from hard work…are both right. Each will have many experiences to prove that their belief about abundance is a fact.

The good news is though…you can change your belief and therefore change your experience. Change your money philosophy and you will change the amount of money flowing to you. This same philosophy applies to any area of your life. What you resonate with is what you will create, and with 100% accuracy.

And, like it or not, what you have now is exactly what you have resonated out to the world and what you have received in return.

One of Jim's latest programs "Cracking the Rich Code" focuses on the subconscious programs influencing one's relationship with money and their financial success.

www.CrackingTheRichCode.com

***

To contact Jim:

Or, for more information on Jim's work:

www.JimBritt.com

www.facebook.com/jimbrittonline

www.linkedin.com/in/jim-britt

www.PowerOfLettingGo.com For free audio series sessions 1&2

Sue Bodine

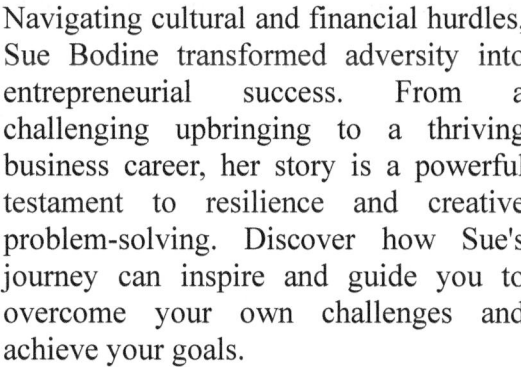

Navigating cultural and financial hurdles, Sue Bodine transformed adversity into entrepreneurial success. From a challenging upbringing to a thriving business career, her story is a powerful testament to resilience and creative problem-solving. Discover how Sue's journey can inspire and guide you to overcome your own challenges and achieve your goals.

Sue Bodine, a business growth coach, author, and keynote speaker, empowers entrepreneurs and coaches to grow their businesses. She helps her clients enhance visibility, define their niches, and master lead generation. Her coaching goes beyond basic strategies, focusing on personal development and overcoming deep-seated barriers to success.

Her comprehensive coaching framework covers critical areas, including:

- Market Clarity: Sharpen your focus for precise market positioning.
- Program Development: Design impactful offerings that resonate with your target audience.
- Sales Strategies: Optimize your pricing and sales techniques for maximum impact.
- Client Acquisition: Broaden your influence and reach.
- Personal Mastery: Cultivate self-belief and overcome your doubts.

With a Master's in Business and certification as a Master Practitioner of NLP, Sue combines strong business acumen with transformative coaching techniques. Her military leadership background and extensive experience in real estate and business provide unique insights into strategic growth.

Discover Sue Bodine's innovative strategies and personal anecdotes in her chapter. Start a journey that not only inspires but also provides a practical guide for achieving success and financial prosperity.

How To Be Your Own Financial Architect: Building Generational Wealth

By Sue Bodine

Imagine waking up one day and realizing that much of what you believe isn't really your own beliefs. This was the moment in my life that changed everything for me. Sounds wild, right? Let me take you back to where it all began.

When I was six, I had no concept of a happy family. My parents' arguments boomed through the house, echoing like thunder. My stepsisters, fifteen years older than me, were far from allies. Despite my youthful innocence, I yearned to belong to their circle, to be part of what seemed like the cool sisters' clan. Yet, no matter how much I wished and tried, I remained on the outside, feeling like an unnoticed, unwanted black sheep.

My stepsisters despised my dad, a strict, bitter alcoholic adhering to traditional Turkish values. These values enforced strict curfews and established a clear hierarchy of who could speak freely in our home, which often silenced even my free-spirited, independent mom.

While growing up, money was a constant visitor at our house, but not the good kind. It was more like an unwelcome guest who wouldn't leave, causing all sorts of trouble. My parents argued about it all the time. And when they divorced, the money problems didn't go away; they lingered, casting a shadow over everything.

My dad, especially, had a tough time with it. He saw money as the root of all evil. To him, it symbolized the harsh injustices of life, reinforcing his belief that those with wealth probably didn't deserve it. After the divorce, my dad and I moved in with my grandparents. We had no choice since my dad could not afford rent and daycare.

I'm deeply grateful to my grandparents for taking us in. However, like my dad, they also struggled with money. My grandpa tracked every penny spent, and it always felt like there was never enough. He was so strict about money that I even had to pay for phone calls to my friends. I was just a kid in middle school with no income. Not being able to call my friends made me feel isolated and left out, making simple social interactions a painful reminder of our financial situation.

As I got older, I started to notice something—I was walking down the same path of chasing after money but never really catching up. Saving money or planning for the future? That felt like something from another planet. My mom wasn't in the picture much, so her perspective on money didn't influence me.

My life changed for the better when I realized our relationship with money, our values around it, and how we see ourselves set the stage for our financial wealth. It hit me—I had been living my dad's and grandparents' money values without realizing it. I was stuck in their world, not mine. These realizations and my breakthrough enabled me to embark on a journey to become a successful real estate investor and business coach, allowing me to quit the rat race.

This breakthrough was more than a financial awakening; it was a profound shift in consciousness, altering how I viewed myself and my capabilities.

In my early corporate career, I struggled with money for a long time without realizing I was missing a crucial piece of the puzzle. I pursued an MBA, thinking climbing the corporate ladder would free me financially. However, this belief wasn't even my own. Growing up, my dad instilled in me that success and financial freedom came from attending college and earning a degree. Society also conditions us to believe that a well-paying job and saving for retirement are the keys to financial freedom. But through my experiences, I soon learned that this is not the whole story.

Following societal expectations, I did exactly what I was conditioned to do—I worked harder, landed a better job, and saved more money, all because I thought that would lead to real financial freedom. But that's not freedom; it's like being stuck in a hamster wheel. Paying 35% in taxes, spending time lamenting about the economy, your boss, or life's frustrations—these actions don't lead to financial freedom. They merely keep you running in circles, trapped in a cycle many of us know all too well.

So, I want to ask you a question: What do you believe about money? Are these beliefs truly yours, or have you adopted them from your family? Understanding your starting point is crucial before progressing to where you want to be. Realizing your beliefs about money is the first step towards a healthy financial relationship. That's why I will share with you how the Graves Model helped me align my values with my financial goals. Trust me; it's a game-changer.

Do you ever ask yourself what it will take to be free from debt or what it will take to stop worrying about bills? It's one thing to talk about wealth, but it's another to lie awake at night, unable to sleep because you've just paid for groceries with your credit card—because you've run out of money, again! The truth is, once we understand our history and what's going on at the subconscious level, we can create a plan for a better future. I want to be clear: creating wealth is possible for anyone willing to do the work, confront their limiting beliefs, and take consistent, strategic actions.

I can attest to this from personal experience. I remember making decent money when I was in the military. It was decent, considering I was single with no bills, held a second job, and had a steady income that could have led to substantial savings. But what did I do with all that money? I blew it on clothes, jewelry, friends... Yeah, I had no clue how to manage my finances. Looking back, it's clear that I needed better spending habits. This lack of discipline reflects a more prominent issue—how deeply we're conditioned to rely on traditional safety net like 401(k)s and Social Security for retirement, without learning the essential skills for managing our money effectively.

The struggle with money continued. When I met my husband, we were both in the military. I left the service to have our daughter while he stayed in. Living on an airman's salary then meant our family of three was below the poverty level. We had to use coupons to buy groceries. I remember the embarrassment of having to pay for food with what felt like fake money. Living the dream, right? In the richest country in the world, and yet one parent can't stay at home to care for their newborn without financial strain. We are taxed so heavily that escaping the cycle of just trying to catch up seems impossible.

Fed up with our endless financial struggles, I was determined to turn things around. Earning my bachelor's degree was my ticket off the 'fake money' wagon. Once we started earning more and actually had some extra cash, guess what happened? We fell into the trap of buying nicer things, ironically just sinking us deeper into debt. We could handle the monthly payments but weren't saving a dime. The golden rule of money management is simple: don't lose what you've earned, and always pay yourself first. But in a society that constantly flashes luxury cars and celebrity lifestyles, resisting the urge to spend more is tough. Television feeds us a version of life that's hard to ignore. This constant exposure makes wanting more feel normal, even addictive, especially when you've battled financial hardship for so long. 'It's okay to indulge,' we tell ourselves. I've been there and know how hard it is to break that cycle.

In our quest for a better future, we knew sticking to day jobs wasn't enough. We ventured into starting side businesses with small investments, aiming to further our financial stability. However, it felt like struggling to swim in a vast ocean against a strong current, constantly being hit by waves, with no one in sight to throw us a life jacket. Eventually, we gave up, resigned to a fate that seemed to dictate we were not meant to be well-off.

Fast-forward about 15 years. In search of ways to help myself, I stumbled upon a gold mine that clarified everything. I often get asked about this pivotal point in my life. So here's what happened: I stopped asking the wrong questions and started asking the right ones. Instead of wondering why everything and everyone around me wasn't working for me or with me, I shifted my focus. I began asking what I could change about myself to help me overcome my financial and personal struggles.

My relentless quest for answers led me into the fields of psychology and the science behind how changing our thoughts can profoundly change our lives. I discovered that our brains function like prediction machines, constantly drawing from past experiences to forecast our future. This insight was pivotal, leading me to a profound breakthrough where I released deep-seated emotional and mental blocks. This transformative experience liberated me from the shackles of my past, empowering me to enjoy my life and success as an entrepreneur. It was an intense journey, marked by moments of revelation and emotional release as I confronted and discarded long standing beliefs of unworthiness—scars left by years of living with an alcoholic father who was consumed by his anger.

Values imposed by others, beliefs about unworthiness, and feelings of being undeserving of love can profoundly alter your life. Experiencing this breakthrough was so transformative that I became certified to guide others through similar transformations. It's more than a process; it's a journey that can fundamentally change your life. As a coach, it's incredibly rewarding to witness my clients break free from the endless cycle of financial struggle and start building lasting wealth.

One of the critical steps in this process is to discard the values and beliefs that don't serve you. Believe me, when you release all that baggage, you start seeing things as they really are. For me, it was as if the clouds parted and I felt the light warming me inside, bringing a sense of wholeness. I did something I never thought possible—I forgave my parents and sisters for everything that had happened. I forgave my dad for all the pain he inflicted on me. I realized that my past no longer held any power over me.

Can you imagine how freeing this is? This realization isn't just about personal liberation; it's about understanding that each of us has the potential to rewrite our stories and reclaim our power.

Remember this: You were born to succeed! Just imagine living without limitations for a moment—how would that change your life? Imagine a reality where your struggles simply fade away, lifting you to a new level of understanding and experience. Witnessing such transformations fills me with immense joy and fulfillment in my coaching practice.

Once we master the inner game, the outer game becomes more manageable. So, ask yourself, what are your values about money? Are they truly yours, or, like me, have you inherited them from someone else or somewhere else? Understanding where we stand is crucial before we can set sail toward where we want to be!

Understanding our values and beliefs about money is the first step toward creating a healthy relationship with it. That's why I'll dive into Clare Graves' model, showing you how to use it to align your values with your financial goals.

Clare W. Graves developed the "Graves Model," a simple way to understand how people grow and change through different stages of their lives. This model affects everything from what we believe to how we handle money. Each stage shows us a different way to see the world.

This isn't just theory; it's practical. For example, understanding your current stage can explain why you're cautious with investments or driven to pursue business opportunities.

Building on Graves' work, Don Beck and Chris Cowan developed Spiral Dynamics, using colors to label these stages. This system makes it easy to understand where you are and discover where you could go next in your personal and financial life.

Why does this matter to you? By understanding this model, you can better navigate your path to financial and personal success. It's like having a GPS for your growth and financial strategies.

Here's a brief overview of these levels:

1. Beige: Focuses on basic survival needs such as food, water, warmth, and safety.
2. Purple: Centers around tribalistic and spiritual beliefs, emphasizing safety provided by spirits, ancestors, and rituals.
3. Red: Characterized by dominance, power, heroic leadership, self-assertion, and control.
4. Blue: Represents order, law, morality, discipline, and obedience to rightful authority.
5. Orange: Describes individuals who are entrepreneurial, opportunistic, success-oriented, and materialistic.
6. Green: Highlights a communitarian, humanistic approach that values community and relationships.
7. Yellow: At this stage, individuals adopt an integrative, holistic view, with contextual thinking and a sense of self-worth that is not tied to material possessions.
8. Turquoise: Defined by a global, holistic, and integrative perspective, where the self is part of a larger consciousness.

Each level represents a distinct worldview with its own set of values. None is superior or inferior to the others; they reflect the diverse ways humans perceive the world.

Now, let's dive deeper into how this model can be employed to align your values with your financial goals:

Identifying Your Level: Recognizing your current level is the first step. This insight provides a valuable understanding of your values and motivations, helping you see what drives your financial decisions. For example, if you're at the Orange level, you might focus on entrepreneurship and personal achievements. Meanwhile, someone at the Green level might prioritize social responsibility and community well-being. This clarity can help you align your financial goals with your true values.

Aligning Financial Goals with Your Level: Once you've identified your level, you can align your goals with your worldview. For example, you might focus on wealth maximization and business expansion at the Orange level. At the Green level, your financial goals could revolve around supporting community initiatives or investing in socially responsible causes.

Understanding the Next Level: As you grow, your values and goals will shift. Knowing the next level in the model can prepare you for these changes. For instance, transitioning from Orange to Green might shift your focus from financial gains to prioritizing environmental and social factors. This foresight helps you adjust your financial strategies in advance.

Seek Personalized Guidance: As I guide my clients through the wealth creation process, I recognize that each person's path is unique. No single piece of advice suits everyone's circumstances, values, and goals. Personalized guidance can be transformative if you're struggling to align your financial goals with your values or if uncertainty clouds your financial future.

In my experience, finding resources, mentors, and learning opportunities that match your current values and understanding is helpful. Books, courses, or seminars that fit well with where you are right now can offer excellent guidance on your financial journey. I recommend working with a coach or mentor who gets your perspective and can give you advice that's just right for you. With the right help, you can get a clear view of your financial goals and make choices that fit your values and where you are in life.

Your journey to financial success is deeply personal, involving a financial reality that aligns with your evolving values, beliefs, and consciousness. Let me share my evolution to illustrate.

It began at the Beige level, where I was focused only on survival and constantly worried about money, just like my family. As I grew and inherited my family's Purple-level values, my loyalty to their financial views deepened, even though they didn't serve my best interests.

Earning my own money propelled me into the Red level, where I sought to control my financial destiny but was still hindered by old beliefs. After earning my MBA and climbing the corporate ladder, I adhered to societal norms at the Blue level—education, a high-paying job, a 401k—but still lacked true financial freedom.

Undergoing the breakthrough process helped me realize that societal norms were not fulfilling. This realization propelled me into the Orange level, where I adopted an entrepreneurial spirit to define my own success. This was not just a step but a leap towards true financial independence.

My journey didn't stop there. As my understanding deepened, I progressed to the Green level, where I recognized the importance of community and began redefining my relationship with money to serve myself and others. This profound transformation marked a pivotal point in my view of financial success—not as individual gain but as collective well-being.

Continued introspection brought me to the Yellow level, where I began to see money as a tool to create the life I desired, not an end goal. Now, advancing towards the Turquoise level, I understand that my financial well-being is part of a larger global consciousness. I aim to align my financial goals with my true values and use my wealth to impact the world positively.

As you can see, each stage of my journey has been a step in aligning my financial strategies with my personal growth. The breakthrough process I experienced and now teach was a turning point that resonates deeply with the themes discussed in this chapter. It's a testament to how you, too, can align your values with your financial goals for generational success and wealth.

So, embrace the journey, seek guidance that resonates, and never forget: your values and personal growth are not just part of your financial future—they shape it. Forge ahead with confidence!

Interested in your own breakthrough?

Schedule a free call here: bit.ly/RichCode-With-Sue

***

To contact Sue:

SueBodine.com

linkedin.com/in/coachsuebodine

facebook.com/sue.b.bodine

NOTE: to Al. Both Tammy and Sylvia have bios on separate pages prior to the chapter they wrote together

Tammy Vallieres

Tammy Vallieres, known as The Hero Intelligence Teacher and Chief Visionary of Raising Empowered Kids, is a transformational educator with over 25 years of experience. Through her roles as a teacher, coach, author, mentor, and consultant, Tammy empowers both adults and children to unlock their true potential, fostering harmonious and inspiring learning environments.

Tammy is the innovative mind behind the Vallieres Method, which encompasses Hero Intelligence Education. This method is designed to guide children in aligning with their purpose, passion, and personalities, nurturing them into compassionate leaders. Utilizing storytelling, critical thinking, adaptability, and resilience, Tammy empowers children to overcome challenges and view life as an opportunity for exploration. She strongly believes in the power of imagination to foster personal and creative growth.

A defining moment in Tammy's journey occurred nineteen years ago when a dove hit her classroom window on Remembrance Day at 11:00 am on 11/11. This event ignited her passion for **Peace Education**, leading her to reshape her entire approach to teaching.

Tammy's exceptional talent lies in harnessing children's superpowers through engaging characters and imaginative stories. Her strengths in positive psychology, understanding the meaning of life, and maintaining an optimistic attitude towards the global vision of creating heaven on earth inspire and empower those around her.

Sylvia Tam

Sylvia Tam is a mompreneur dedicated to assisting parents in nurturing entrepreneurial habits for their children's three super brains - head, heart, and gut. As a mother of three teenpreneurs, Sylvia's passion is to promote creativity, kindness, and healthy habits in families. She often reflects that raising teens has been the most rewarding part of her parenting journey.

As Chief Strategist at Raising Empowered Kids, Sylvia supports parents through innovative resources, engaging kids' camps, and comprehensive courses and workshops. Drawing from her diverse expertise, she ignites ideas and confidence in educators as Director of Education at Kidpreneurs, where she trains and coaches educators worldwide to launch educational businesses.

Sylvia also leads teen volunteer initiatives and builds communities through her podcast *Mompreneurs Raising Kidpreneurs* and events. Sylvia is additionally a startup and parenting consultant, founder, and food innovator at Beviva Foods, and a certified habit coach. A sought-after speaker on purposeful parenting, Sylvia shares her insights to inspire and educate parents on the many life-changing benefits of instilling an entrepreneurial mindset in youth.

Raising Empowered Kids with Hero Intelligence
Our Mission & Methodology

By Tammy Vallieres & Sylvia Tam

Picture a world where every child radiates confidence, tackles challenges with unwavering determination, and embraces the future with boundless optimism.

Welcome to Raising Empowered Kids, where we don't just dream of such a world—we make it a reality. Through our groundbreaking and holistic Hero Intelligence Approach, by Tammy Vallieres, we ignite the spark of potential in every child. We empower them to conquer obstacles, embrace opportunities, and emerge as compassionate leaders of tomorrow.

Hero Intelligence (HQ) = IQ (Intelligence) + EQ (Emotional) + SQ (Social) + GQ (Genius) + AQ (Adaptability)

Our mission is clear: to foster not only intelligence but resilience, and not just capability, but kindness. We're committed to nurturing a generation that's emotionally resilient, socially aware, and morally grounded. Alongside teaching life, learning, and leadership skills, we strive to cultivate well-rounded individuals poised for success in all aspects of life.

The Hero Intelligence teaching model emphasizes understanding the interplay of our three shadows - the Hero, Victim, and Villain - within us all. We teach children as young as kindergarten to be aware of these shadows, empowering them to let their hero become the leader of their life.

This philosophy takes a deeper dive into personal growth and development, focusing on the power of five Super Identities: the Dreamer, the Guardian, the Magician, the Royal, and the Hero. Teaching these concepts from an early age sets a foundation for lifelong social and emotional intelligence.

Once children grasp the concepts of their inner world through our Hero Intelligence model, we provide them with stories, tips, tools, and guides for navigating the outer world. Using the Compass of Life and our Animal Guides from A to F, such as Annie the Ant, who teaches about Attitude and Altitude, or Ellie the Elephant, who represents Energy and Emotions, we equip them with practical wisdom for their journey ahead.

Our Power of Three

Get ready to explore how Sylvia Tam, Tammy Vallieres, and the dynamic duo Adam and Matthew Toren come together to transform education in home, school, and career. Together, they create a tapestry of purposeful parenting, hero intelligence teaching, and youth entrepreneurship, guiding you through a holistic approach to raising empowered kids.

I AM THE PURPOSEFUL PARENT
Sylvia Tam, Upland, California

"Life's not about waiting for the storm to pass, it's learning to dance in the rain."

– Vivian Greene

My Dream: Revolutionizing Parenting for a Better World

In the midst of managing a health food business, raising three kids, and managing my digestive disease, I sensed an unfulfilled longing. It felt as though I was torn between the worlds of parenting and entrepreneurship. Then, in 2020, during a period of deep introspection, the ikigai method revealed an unexpected truth: my purpose lay in advocating for "parentpreneurs." Drawing from a lifetime of experiences—from teaching at a young age to running a national STEM camp—I founded Mompreneurs Raising Kidpreneurs. Through this community, podcast, and events, I aim to create conversations and support networks for parents, debunking the myth that parenting teenagers is the hardest phase. My goal is to help every family experience a happy, healthy, and harmonious relationship with their children.

My Superpower: Igniting Dreams with Creativity

My calling discovery, rooted in igniting both children's and adults' dreams, perfectly complements the essence of purposeful parenting. Learning from past business ventures, I've honed the skill of guiding individuals towards turning their passions into thriving ventures, instilling them with an entrepreneurial mindset. This journey has been deeply intertwined with raising my three teens, where I witnessed firsthand the transformative impact of igniting their passions. As I expanded my reach, I found success in working with small businesses, Kidpreneurs certified educators, and eventually in larger group settings like Camp SuperNova.

Since crossing paths with my partners, Tammy Vallieres, and Adam and Matthew Toren, my superpower found its perfect application. Our connection began serendipitously: my involvement in educational training naturally led me to Tammy, while my son's engagement with Kidpreneurs introduced us to the Toren brothers. United by our shared passion for empowering children and families, our bond grew stronger over time, culminating in our collaboration, Raising Empowered Kids.

My Message: The Power of Habits and the Three Brains

During my research into creating products at Beviva Foods, I stumbled upon a remarkable revelation: the existence of three interconnected brains—head, heart, and gut—and their influence on one another. This discovery formed the cornerstone of my parenting method, focusing on nurturing healthy habits and resilient relationships to support children's overall well-being.

In conversations with hundreds of thriving mompreneurs, insights into the intricate dynamics of parenting and entrepreneurship emerged. Each brain—head for creativity and productivity, heart for kindness and mindfulness, and gut for health and wellness—plays a pivotal role in this dynamic. These discussions ignited my curiosity about human behavior, leading me to pursue certified training in habits and behavior. Coaching individuals to adopt habits tailored to their three brain areas has proven to be incredibly rewarding, offering a pathway to positive change. My message emphasizes the art of habit-building as the foundation for purposeful parenting.

My Heroes: Learning from the True Champions in My Life

Mine aren't the ones in capes. They're the ones who anchor me when life gets stormy, and who I'm blessed to call my children.

Ben, always sticking to his healthy habits, keeps me grounded in taking care of myself. His commitment to staying active and eating well reminds me of the importance of looking after my own well-being.

Viani, bold and brave, shows me how to embrace new things without fear. Whether it's changing schools or learning something new, her adventurous spirit teaches me the power of curiosity and courage.

And then there's **Va**nessa, empathetic and aware of others, who shows me how to bounce back from tough times. Her kindness and ability to manage difficult emotions gracefully inspire me to be more understanding in my own life.

I named my business Beviva to honor them, with our kangaroo mascot symbolizing strength, adaptability, and boundless energy. These youth heroes light up my world and remind me that greatness isn't found in grand gestures but in the small, consistent acts of love and kindness.

My Advice to Parents: Cultivate Entrepreneurial Mindsets Early

I never would have thought that my purple sweet potato snack line, PURPO, would turn into my parenting philosophy. What started as a focus on gut health evolved into a holistic approach to raising kids. PURPO stands for Peaceful, Understanding, Respect Your Genius, Playful, and Opportunistic. By emphasizing these values, I've helped kids build good habits and embrace their unique talents, lighting up as their best selves.

Think of parenting as a journey: start with a solid foundation of respect, responsibility, and authenticity. Be intentional in your actions and communication. Maintain peace, be understanding, honor your child's unique genius, stay playful, and always seek growth opportunities. With this support and guidance, your kids can develop their unique talents and shine brightly. When approached with love and intentionality, parenting can be as fulfilling and rewarding as any entrepreneurial venture. "Their best mentor is YOU."- Sylvia Tam

I AM THE HERO INTELLIGENCE TEACHER

Tammy Vallieres, Woodstock, Ontario Canada

"Somewhere inside all of us is the power to change the world." — Roald Dahl

My Dream: Crafting a Classroom Paradise

Imagine a world where every child is a shining star, destined for greatness. In this dream, every child is cherished, classrooms are peaceful, and learning is an exciting journey of self-discovery and empowerment. Picture classrooms filled with warmth and encouragement, where kids feel safe to explore their passions and express themselves freely, guided by caring adults helping them find their unique path.

This dream isn't just professional for me—it's personal. As a child, I faced challenges in the traditional school system. With support from mentors and my own resilience, I discovered my superpower:

teaching. Now, I create the captivating classrooms I wish I had, ensuring every child knows they are valued, seen, and capable of greatness.

A Turning Point: From Pain to Purpose

A dove hit my window on Remembrance Day at 11:00 am on 11/11. This life-changing moment, 19 years ago, ignited my mission and vision for **Peace Education**, now my life's purpose and calling. It began with a book called *Jeffrey Finds His Way*, then *The Compassionate Crew Assembly Program*, a school-wide initiative, co-created with dedicated partners, teachers, and students, and now includes *Kindergarten Masterclass*. These stories and character development programs give children tools and vision for their future.

My Superpower: Classroom Transformations

Welcome to Kindergarten Masterclass, a 50-minute scaffolding program I co-created to help children become the best they can be. This isn't just a wish but my everyday reality. Here, teachers and students are superheroes with invisible capes, embarking on a journey fueled by passion, purpose, and hidden talents. Kindergarten Masterclass goes beyond traditional education, incorporating kind leadership and self-regulation into every lesson, amplifying each child's unique voice and natural-born gifts.

The Vision: Chaos to Calm

At the heart of the Kindergarten Masterclass is a vision to transform early education into an extraordinary adventure with strategies that support success. I designed each 50-minute period to ignite curiosity and foster creativity, turning classrooms into vibrant spaces where learning is a joyful, harmonious, and engaging experience for everyone.

Superheroes in the Classroom

In Kindergarten Masterclass, every teacher and student is a superhero, authoring their own life's story. Their invisible capes symbolize boundless potential and unfolding chapters of growth. HQ educators lead with their inner child, creating a playful environment where students communicate, collaborate, and contribute to the overall community. By mastering self-regulation and social-emotional intelligence, children become resilient and develop self-control—skills that benefit them throughout their entire lives.

My Message: The World Needs Your Hero

"Imagine if kids ruled the world!" With their energy, intuition, creativity, and compassion, they could achieve amazing things. Every thoughtful word and dream can shape the world. They might not look like heroes on the big screen, but they have special superpowers.

Think of an animal school—each creature, from the tiniest ant to the majestic elephant, brings unique strengths. Similarly, every child has something special to offer. Empowering them to work together can transform their world and ours.

Mother Earth needs everyday heroes ready to act. From Greta Thunberg's climate action to Malala Yousafzai's fight for girls' education, one person can change the world. But it's not just about them. It's about you. Your actions, no matter how small, can create ripples of change. Volunteering, speaking out, or mentoring—these acts of heroism strengthen communities. The world needs your generosity, courage, and compassion.

My Heroes: Real and Fictional

From where I stand, kids are the true champions, teaching and inspiring everyone around them—they've become my master teachers. With their compassion, curiosity, forgiveness, determination, and problem-solving skills, they are the little geniuses from whom we can learn so much. I admire real heroes like Autumn Peltier, who advocates for clean water, and fictional ones like Harry Potter, who stayed true to his humble personality.

Each child has the power to make a big difference through their authenticity and inner strength. They remind us that heroism isn't just about grand gestures; it's in the small, brave acts of compassion we see every day. With over eight billion people in the world, if everyone did just one thing to help, we could solve any problem instantly.

Kid Power is real.

My Advice to Teachers: Empower Children to Shine

When you expect the best from children, the best shows up. As their greatest influencers, we hold the power to shape and inspire their identities and worldviews. The Vallieres Method includes Hero Intelligence Education and the STAR System (Stories, Thinking, Adaptability, and Resilience). It draws from over 25 years of teaching experience and wisdom from masters like Rudolf Steiner and Joseph Campbell, plus insights from personal growth and development giants like Tony Robbins, Roger Hamilton, and Vishen Lakhiani.

Remember, self-worth begins with how we speak to children. Our words become their inner voice. Let's be positive role models, fostering encouragement and igniting their love of life and learning.

"The Hero in Me Sees The Hero in YOUth." — Tammy Vallieres

WE ARE THE BUSINESS BROTHERS

Adam Toren, Phoenix, Arizona

Matthew Toren, Vancouver, British Columbia

"The best way to predict the future is to create it." — Peter Drucker

Our Dream: Empower Entrepreneurial Futures

From a young age, we dreamed of building businesses that not only succeeded but also made a difference in the world. Growing up, our grandfather, Joe, inspired us and introduced us to the world of entrepreneurship. Now, our dream is to empower individuals of all ages to pursue their entrepreneurial passions. We believe that entrepreneurship is a path to personal and financial freedom, and it has the power to transform lives and communities.

Our Superpower: Vision and Resilience

Our journey has been marked by our ability to see potential where others see obstacles. This vision, coupled with our resilience, has been our superpower. Whether it was turning around a struggling billiard hall or creating one of the largest online communities for entrepreneurs, our vision guided us. Resilience allowed us to persevere through challenges and setbacks. We've always believed that failure is not the end but a steppingstone to success. Each setback provided valuable lessons that helped us grow and improve.

Our Message: Bridging the Accessibility Gap in Entrepreneurship

We have dedicated our lives to spreading the message that entrepreneurship is within reach for everyone. Through our books, *Small Business, Big Vision*, *Kidpreneurs*, and *Real World Money Lessons* as well as our online platforms and personal mentorship, we aim to inspire and educate. Our mission is to provide aspiring entrepreneurs with the tools, knowledge, and confidence they need to start, manage, and grow successful businesses. We believe that by sharing our experiences and insights, we can help others avoid common pitfalls and achieve their dreams.

Our Heroes: Family Roots of Inspiration

Adam: My hero is my grandfather, Joe. He was a true entrepreneur who taught us the value of hard work, perseverance, and creativity. His influence is evident in every venture we undertake. He instilled in us the belief that with determination and innovative thinking, we can overcome any challenge.

Matthew: For me, our mother is my hero. Her unwavering support and belief in our potential were crucial in our journey. She taught us to dream big, stay resilient, and never give up, no matter how tough things get. Her lessons in resilience and optimism have guided us through the ups and downs of entrepreneurship.

Our Advice to Parent Entrepreneurs: Nurturing Your Business and Family

Balancing parenthood and entrepreneurship is no small feat, but it's incredibly rewarding. Here are some tips based on our experiences:

1. *Involve Your Kids:* Engage your children in your business activities. This not only teaches them valuable skills but also fosters a sense of responsibility and entrepreneurship. It can be as simple as explaining what you do or involving them in small tasks.
2. *Time Management*: Effective time management is crucial. Prioritize your tasks and use tools and techniques that help you balance your business and family life. Set clear boundaries and allocate specific times for work and family.
3. *Lead by Example:* Demonstrate the values of hard work, perseverance, and ethical business practices. Your children learn by observing you. Show them how to manage successes and setbacks gracefully.
4. *Seek Support:* Don't hesitate to seek help from family, friends, or professional networks. Building a support system is vital for maintaining balance and ensuring that neither your family nor your business suffers.
5. *Self-Care*: Take care of yourself. Entrepreneurship can be demanding, and it's easy to burn out. Make sure to set aside time for relaxation and self-care. A healthy mind and body are essential for maintaining productivity and balance.
6. *Be Present*: When you're with your family, be fully present. It's important to have quality time with your loved ones without distractions. This helps in building strong family bonds and ensures that your children feel valued and supported.

Our entrepreneurial journey has been filled with learning, growth, and a passion for helping others succeed. We believe in the transformative power of entrepreneurship and are committed to sharing our knowledge and experiences to inspire future generations. Through our work, we hope to create a lasting impact and encourage others to pursue their dreams with determination and resilience.

Whether you're starting your first venture or your tenth, remember that with the right mindset and support, anything is possible.

Final Thoughts

Reflecting on our journey, we are grateful for the opportunities and experiences that have shaped us. From our early days of selling stunt airplanes to creating influential online communities, every step has been a learning experience. We are proud of the businesses we've built and the impact we've had on the entrepreneurial community. Our story is a testament to the power of vision, resilience, and unwavering support from loved ones. As we continue to mentor and inspire, we remain committed to our dream of empowering the next generation of entrepreneurs.

"It's never too early to start." — The Toren Brothers

Our North Star - To Educate, Elevate, and Empower

As a transformative education media company, REK is committed to redefining education and creating a brighter future for all children. Our collective vision is rooted in the belief that every child deserves to be empowered, celebrated, and equipped with the tools to thrive in an ever-changing world. Through our dedication and innovative approaches, we are shaping a new narrative —one that celebrates diversity, fosters creativity, and cultivates resilience.

Be part of a community that shapes the next generation of leaders, thinkers, and changemakers. Here's how:

- Subscribe to our *Roots to Wings* newsletter at: join.raisingempoweredkids.com.
- Take our Shadow Identity Assessment at: myshadow.raisingempoweredkids.com.
- Download our HQ Dreamer Kit at: dream.raisingempoweredkids.com.
- Explore our events at: raisingempoweredkids.com.

We invite you to raise empowered kids who will shape the future of our world. Let's unlock the limitless potential within every child and pave the way for a brighter tomorrow.

***

To contact Tammy and Sylvia:

https://linktr.ee/raisingempoweredkids

hello@raisingempoweredkids.com

689-244-4332

Connect with Tammy on Facebook
https://www.facebook.com/tammy.vallieres.14

or LinkedIn ww.linkedin.com/in/tammy-vallieres-a5887690/

Sallyann A. Martinez

Sallyann A. Martinez is a dynamic public speaker, author, and accomplished business professional known for embracing new challenges with vision and creativity. Her corporate career began in New York City, where she excelled in advertising and marketing. Sallyann led successful projects for lifestyle and consumable clients in fashion, restaurant, and beverage industries, both domestically and internationally. She worked with the largest advertising agency and a prominent Manhattan-based restaurant, pioneered multi-tiered client collaborations with Madison Square Garden, and orchestrated cross-promotion events with the Knicks, Rangers, and Yankees. Additionally, she managed international accounts, helping Pepsi launch as a mixer in 18 countries and developing concepts for various liquor brands.

After relocating to Arizona, Sallyann founded and managed a successful theater company that remains profitable 20 years later. She also created programs and promotions for a major retail development, integrating her philanthropic passions with effective marketing strategies that boosted overall profitability for the brand and its tenants. Many of her innovative marketing techniques are still widely used today.

Sallyann's overarching philosophy is one of light, love, and knowledge aimed at making the world a better place with better humans. Following her passion, she began this new chapter in her life by leaving a corporate job to establish Heaven's Light Wellness. Sallyann is committed to guiding people toward living their best lives through focused energy and empowerment. She is the author of *The Empowerment Approach* and *Empowerment through Gratitude* both dedicated to enriching the lives of others.

The Empowerment of Finding Yourself...A Letter to Myself

By Sallyann Angerami Martinez

Trust Yourself...always trust yourself! Those are the first and last words I would have told myself years ago when I was starting Heavens Light Wellness and ultimately The Empowerment Approach. It has been eight wonderful years of growing and knowing and finding and helping. I had to *look* and *feel* and *trust* to be where we are today.

Let's start at the beginning of the end. After almost a decade of managing a large retail environment that was clearly coming to an end. I felt the difference in the air. The energy was different all around me. It is hard to explain but I think you have the essence of what I mean. You feel the energy shift. You feel when things are happy and when things are strained. We feel it in our everyday lives: at the grocery store or work or even in our own homes. And well, you Sallyann, were definitely feeling it at work. And so, you did what any other human would do that was working for a company... you sent your resume out and started interviewing for another job. But first you had to look at yourself in a different way. And it was an interesting view.

At that time, your job was such a major focus of your life. It almost defined who you were. Almost. It was funny because we were on the cutting edge of social media and were one of the first to start using the "new platform" of Facebook for the retail environment. And as the Marketing Director I needed to create a personal account. As you might recall, you need to write a short summary of who you are for the front of your page to introduce yourself. It was hard to write 20 words about who I was. It initially started with ...Marketing Director, successful NYC Account Manager, founder of a theatre company. But then I stopped short. I looked at those words and realized that was what I did. Not who I was. I was a mom, and proud of it. I was a wife and a sister and a friend and an adventure seeker and a shower singer who liked to laugh and enjoy the people around me. That was who I was. And that was the first time I looked at myself through a different lens and it helped me grow. I felt a little taller when I was able to write my real truth. At only 5'3" I will take anything that makes me feel taller…

I reviewed my resume. I actually looked at it and knew it was such an expansive part of my life. Such wonderful opportunities that I took and breathed life into. Every opportunity was an experience of learning and challenging myself to be better and to learn more. All the people I was blessed to work with taught me so so much. Abundantly more than what the job description listed. The New York City experience is what helped me become the professional and person I was today. And the knowledge and experience were profound. What I was most proud of, however, was that people I worked with this past decade used words to describe me as fair, intelligent, all-encompassing thinker, strategic and kind. I have always strived for a win-win situation with any partnerships I entered. Again, I looked at myself with new eyes and while I might have blushed from the compliments, I realized that it had the power of truth.

The end of the end happens… I was called into an office and given an envelope and was told thank you for your tenure but that your salary could no longer be sustained with the new business model that was evolving in the current economy. I chuckled at my Vice President. I literally gave a short laugh out loud, not disrespectfully but with understanding. I said "good luck" to them, stood up tall and walked out of their office door to pack up my office of personal possessions collected over the ten years of 60-hour work weeks. It was oddly freeing. I knew it was coming. I thought I was prepared. I really did feel sorry for the organization. I was, of course, replaceable but I knew I was amazingly good at what I did. And secretly I was not worried about finding a new job. I had multiple contacts in the industry and was respected. The phone started to ring almost immediately as the word spread and I was literally packing up my office.

And then the Universe kicked my butt….6 weeks later and no job. I was dumbfounded. How could this happen? How do you know the mayor of a town and not be able to get a job interview for a marketing position for that town? How do you know the Vice President and Directors and managers at the largest radio station and not get the opportunity to work as a promotion's person? How do you collaborate with a supplier for ten years and not get a call to fill a position you are perfect for? And so that continued and the count grew of oddly missed job opportunities. Yes, it was true. I was feeling discouraged and sorry for myself. I was surprised and so were those that I knew in the corporate world. I was the most employable person they knew. But the Universe had a different plan for me. *I had to feel this one.*

I was with a friend of mine that had terrible foot pain. She had plantar fasciitis and asked me to do some Reiki and energy healing on her to help her stand and heal. Of course I agreed. It was one of the things I loved to do with my spiritual gifts, and I was a Reiki Master. I had been doing angel readings and energy healing for almost 30 years for friends and family. So, it was not out of the question that I would work on my dear friend. And then she asked the magic question. "How are you?" …ugh.

Well, I started to tell her of all the job opportunities that just seemed to be whisked away. Job after job I counted and recounted the perceived opportunities. And as I got to listing the last two, visually using my fingers to count… my eyes grew playful, and the darkness went away. My voice got higher with amusement, and I took a deep yoga style breath. I started to laugh. Ha. Thirteen opportunities. Of course, the number 13. How could I not have seen it. But the Universe needed to hit me in the face and make me feel it with this magical Sallyann number so I would know…

Let me fill you in on the number thirteen. While for some, it is a foreboding number, I consider it my lucky number. First, I got married on the 13th. Married in the middle of summer on a hot Arizona day. I most certainly did not want to get married in 125-degree weather, but the Universe started its plan of making thirteen my favorite number. Our best man was coming in from Germany and he had a certain window of time. When we went to the church, they only had a Saturday available. So, thirteen was when we became a couple.

Three years later my son decided to make an appearance two weeks early. "This baby could play linebacker for the Jets" said the doctor after an emergency c-section. He showed up on Friday the 13th in a big and extreme way. He made us a beautiful joy filled family.

Five years later my little girl shows up on her terms, just the way she lives life. She is two days early and she flies into this world fast, almost without the doctor. I still remember the panic in the nurses' voice as she screams into the intercom, "Doctor Stat!". Two pushes and she was in the world ready to make a difference. Surprise, that was also on the 13th. Not only did we become a couple and a family, but we became each other's reasons for smiling; reason for being on this planet; reason for loving and laughing; reason for living a full life. How could the number 13 be anything but my lucky and blessed number. The Universe was clearly showing me something.

So, you can imagine why I started to smile when I realized thirteen work opportunities had not come to fruition. I looked at my girlfriend with awe and shock after I recounted the number of opportunities that did not happen. She looked at me very nonchalantly, shrugged her shoulders and said, as only a fellow New Yorker could say, "Well you're doing what you're supposed to be do anyway. I don't know why you're looking elsewhere". My mouth opened, my brain cleared, *and I could feel my purpose.* It was a profound moment! And it is where it started.

And now to trust myself…Ahhh, the hardest and most rewarding part of the journey! Spoiler alert… You will affect other humans in a positive way. You will live a life free of fear and anxiety. You will create a space for the work you love to do. You will have a full and rich life.

It is a process... That will be one of your mantras. It will hold true for you and for your clients. The full process will accumulate in bits and pieces. About every two years a part of the process will become so clear. Like a shiny gift of clarity to hold deep inside. It will show itself again and again and again until you can break the amazing code to share with everyone that will listen. It is the Empowerment Approach.

And trusting yourself and your intuition is the first of the four steps of this process, called the Empowerment Approach. The business journey starts with small groups where you meet people and share your story. You trust yourself and your unique talents for communicating with angels and the healing. Recognize this is a true gift entrusted to you by the Universe to help others.' It is frightening to be that vulnerable, but it is essential. Those intimate gatherings allow people the opportunity to see their authentic self. Those that attend let their guard down, trust you and become your clients. Without needing to advertise, your clientele grows through referrals. Those who need your guidance always find you when they need you most. The Universe works in your favor.

Within a short amount of time, you have clients across the United States and Internationally. You start with English speaking countries of England, Ireland and Australia. You decide that in order to fulfill your goal of helping a million people trust their intuition, you must test yours. You believe that angel messages will appear if a person trusts themselves and their desires. By opening their intuition, they can receive the positive messages they need. However, we humans need something tangible to hold as proof. This leads to the creation of Angel Empowerment Message cards, a vital part of the trust and awareness process.

At first, you diligently search for quotes and jot down words, approaching the task with professionalism for months. Then, you type everything up, but the results feel off. Without regret, because you just know... You erase it all, knowing it wasn't right yet. And then you just wait. A few days later, you feel inspired and sit at your laptop perched on your blue dining room table. You take a deep breath and as if magic happens, from your fingertips flow 64 beautifully worded positive affirmation messages from the angels. They are so graceful you are sure they are heaven-sent. Clients and friends who use these cards are amazed by how perfectly the messages support them at that moment in time when they draw an empowered angel card message. Listening to yourself and your intuition is another way of trusting yourself.

Once you trust yourself, what do you do with the information? Step two shows up with a retrospective of what you think you know... "With knowledge comes responsibility." This quote has always been a driving life force for you. It can be a double-edged sword. Stress and anxiety can grow with too much information or not enough. Ha! So how do you deal with it. Self-awareness is the key...

If I rest my hands in front of me, they rest at my heart. I like the visual of T-REX arms. They're protecting the very center of my system. Where all information and feelings come into my body and my heart. That special area is where I decide if what is being thrown, handed, given to me in actually all mine and my responsibility. Is it really an icky black blob dressed up like something beautiful? With my T-REX arms I can look at an emotional comment and decide if it all belongs to me. I give myself permission to look at it. Really look at. This is part of the process. I then can take the part that is my responsibility and see the remaining emotions and words belong to the other person and non-ceremoniously toss it aside, so as not to affect me. The rest is not for me to hold. It is not for me to store this non-truth. *I need to feel the truth, my truth.*

Walking thru the gratitude door... You love to say that the door opens in front of you for a reason and you need to walk thru that door/opportunity to gain experience or understand something new. And, because you trust yourself you are able to see and feel gratitude every day. Even with long lines, red lights, and situations you would not choose for loved ones. You know that the way you look at the items and situations in your life with gratitude is your secret key of finding the love and light in life. While gratitude is scientifically proven to change your brain for the better, it is also a beautiful gift to yourself. I can pull it up anytime, any day and have a moment in gratitude to feel the wonders that have been gifted to me. Those moments belong to just me. Those moments help me feel my joy, resilience and value.

Balance... While I love this word it also brings back the terror of a four-year-old on the playground balance beam. Could I cross this 4-inch-wide tenuous path of wood and succeed? I need perspective. The sliding scale of priority is the key. As a woman of my generation, I was told I could have it all. And I wanted it all with balance, vigor and grace. Now, many years into this amazing life, I realize that having it all doesn't mean having it all at ONCE. That implication was always there, however. A life affirming goal without the tools or clarity had become my blind mission. Be a good employee, wife, mother, granddaughter, sister, nurturer, neighbor, volunteer, cheer leader, boss, cook and look/act fabulous *all at the same time*. Exhausting and not sustainable. Yes, continue to have goals. 100% but I needed new direction.

I have broken the code for all of us! First by giving yourself permission not to do everything simultaneously. Then, by shifting your perspective of the moment. I call life this tool of observation and awareness the Sliding Scale of Priority. Every day. Every Hour. Sometimes every 5 minutes my priorities can change. This is not haphazard; it is liberating. It allows me to recognize that, at this moment, I am nurturing my need for self-care, or being a good parent, or listening to a friend, or being a confidant, or being a diligent employee. This sliding scale of perspective is a beautiful way of being present in your life. It gives you the bandwidth to be the person you want to be without the guilt of not having it all at once. Take a breath and acknowledge who you are and what you are doing right now. Understand this is a choice and what I am gaining from this interaction. Also, comprehend that in a few minutes, things can change, and you are leading that change for a better human existence.

So today, yes, at this moment, the empowerment journey and its approach to life seeps into your everyday life. It is most certainly a choice - a daily choice to live in gratitude and be strong enough not to accept others' burdens. Some days, the choice is easy and flows naturally. Other times, you might have to reflect on the last few days or weeks and realize you are not yourself. Where is the joy? That is totally acceptable. Life ebbs and flows…. So, you go back to breathing. And you go back to gratitude. And you go back to understanding your power and you use the four tools that have gotten you here. And you find that you are indeed breaking the rich code. Your life is full and rich in people and experiences and what you want it to be. It has been an extraordinary journey, so far, being open enough to really look at yourself and give yourself permission to feel your feelings. Most importantly, and I will repeat myself from the beginning, is to trust yourself. Congratulations for today and for tomorrow! You got this!

If you are reading this and want to understand the tools of the empowerment approach and/or start on the journey of finding yourself, getting unstuck and becoming unstoppable with a life of trusting your intuition, gratitude, acceptance and personal power, please contact, Sallyann at www.TheEmpowermentApproach.com

Remember in a world where you can be anything, be kind... especially to yourself.

***

To contact Sallyann:

www.TheEmpowermentApproach.com

www.HeavensLightWellness.com, all Social media applications are HeavensLightWellness

Yolanda Martinez

Yolanda Martinez is an evolutionary work in progress, just like you! Yolanda has a unique approach to feminine leadership. She believes in confidently showing up slowly because she will be noticed, and her impact is huge when she does it. Her story did not begin here. Yolanda was born in Apatzingán, Michoacán, Mexico. Yolanda was born in Apatzingán, Michoacán, Mexico. She grew up in Oregon and Washington, where she worked as a migrant worker with her family from 7 until she graduated from High School. Her father taught her the value of money and self-respect. After high school, her parents divorced, and her mother moved the family to Northern California. Believing in pursuing her dreams, Yolanda ventured off on her own to LA at the age of 20. Yolanda's adventures began in LA, where she was in the education industry for 10 years and in the fashion industry for over 25 years. Yolanda is a certified Makeup Artist who loves giving back by empowering and helping women get back into the workforce to help them be independent and positive role models worldwide. Today, Yolanda is an exceptional role model she helps women find their inner power by teaching them the value of self-care, self-love, and self-worth. She is the creator of 21 Days with Yolanda, an online program that touches on those elements. She celebrates her clients every day, but beyond that, she celebrates their lives, self-determination, love stories, and womanhood. Yolanda can't be accurately described in a short biography; she is a mystery that pays to uncover. She makes you feel; she inspires you to soar; she helps you evolve, and she is right by your side.

The Foundation of Female Empowerment

By Yolanda Martinez

In my journey of honoring myself, I discovered that people would treat you the way they see you treat yourself. Growing up, I always saw my mother taking care of everything and everyone but not herself. So, in watching that, as I got older, I realized that I had two choices: I could do what my mother always tried to instill in me, which was that a woman always takes care of the home, the kids, and her husband, or I could stand up for myself, use my voice and follow my own path. My journey of female empowerment was multi-faceted, encompassing personal growth, professional achievements, and the cultivation of healthy relationships. While my individual determination was extremely important, societal progress also played a crucial role, one that I often felt was a misrepresentation of the role that women should have. These factors greatly impacted my positive, healthy, and authentic relationships, which cannot be overstated. These connections serve as a fertile ground for women to blossom into powerful, confident individuals who recognize and embrace their inherent worthiness of success.

The Power of Positive Relationships:

My positive role models were few; growing up, I knew very few women in power, especially none that looked like me. So, for me, Positive romantic, familial, or platonic relationships played a pivotal role in honoring my own empowerment. They provide a safe and nurturing space for me and for women to explore their potential, take risks, and step outside of their comfort zones. The encouragement and belief from loved one's act as a catalyst, propelling women towards their goals with unwavering confidence.

Research has shown that positive relationships are not just beneficial; they are profound. They deeply impact mental and emotional well-being, providing women with a sense of being loved, valued, and appreciated. This flourishing self-esteem and strong sense of self-worth enable women to navigate challenges with resilience, overcome self-doubt, and embrace their unique strengths and abilities. In these relationships, women are not just supported; they are cherished.

In positive relationships, women also find a safe space for vulnerability and authenticity. They can openly express their fears, insecurities, and dreams without fear of judgment or criticism. This emotional intimacy fosters a deep sense of connection and belonging, which in turn fuels personal growth and empowerment. When women feel seen and heard for who they truly are, **it ignites a transformative process. They** are more likely to embrace their individuality, pursue their passions, and achieve their full potential.

The Importance of Healthy Boundaries:

Early on, I learned the importance of having positive friends who help you be a better version of yourself. I also learned that nurturing relationships is just as important as friendship. Positive relationships are crucial, but so are healthy boundaries. These boundaries are not just lines; they're the standards that define acceptable and unacceptable behavior within a relationship. They ensure that you are treated with respect, dignity, and equality, setting the tone for a relationship that is truly beneficial for both parties.

Healthy boundaries are not just about setting limits; they empower women to prioritize their needs and well-being without feeling guilty or selfish. They create a sense of autonomy and control, allowing women to make decisions that align with their values and goals. When women have the freedom to express their opinions, set limits, and protect their personal space, they cultivate a sense of empowerment that extends to all areas of their lives, making them feel validated and important.

Healthy boundaries are not just about you; they're about the relationship. They foster mutual respect and understanding, creating a space where conflicts are less likely to arise. When both parties are clear about their expectations and limits, communication becomes more open and honest. This creates a positive and supportive environment where both partners can thrive and achieve their full potential.

Authenticity as a Catalyst for Empowerment:

Authenticity is the cornerstone of female empowerment. When women embrace their true selves, they tap into a wellspring of inner strength and confidence. Authentic relationships, where women feel safe to be vulnerable and express their genuine thoughts and feelings, play a vital role in fostering this self-acceptance.

In authentic relationships, women are not afraid to be different, to challenge societal norms, or to pursue unconventional paths. They are encouraged to embrace their unique quirks, talents, and perspectives. This freedom of self-expression allows women to discover their true passions, tap into their creativity, and live a life that is aligned with their authentic selves.

Authenticity also breeds resilience. When women are true to themselves, they are less likely to be swayed by external pressures or expectations. They develop a strong sense of self-worth that is not dependent on external validation. This inner strength enables women to navigate challenges, overcome setbacks, and persevere in the face of adversity.

Breaking Free from Limiting Beliefs:

Many women have internalized limiting beliefs about their worthiness of success. Often rooted in societal conditioning and past experiences, these beliefs can hold women back from achieving their full potential. Positive, healthy, and authentic relationships can play a crucial role in dismantling these limiting beliefs. Growing up as a migrant worker, I never believed that my future was only limited to being a migrant worker. I always had bigger dreams and bigger ideas of what my future would be.

When women are surrounded by individuals who believe in them and their abilities, they begin to internalize those positive messages. The constant encouragement and support from loved ones can help women challenge their self-doubt and replace negative self-talk with empowering affirmations.

Moreover, healthy relationships provide a safe space for women to explore their fears and insecurities. Through open and honest communication, women can gain a deeper understanding of the root causes of their limiting beliefs. This self-awareness empowers women to challenge these beliefs, reframe their thoughts, and create new narratives that align with their goals and aspirations.

The Ripple Effect of Female Empowerment:

When I got into teaching, I became aware of the impact I was making and how powerful that was. I feel that when women become empowered, the effects ripple outwards, impacting their families, communities, and society. When women are empowered, they are more likely to advocate for their rights, challenge gender inequality, and create positive change in the world. They serve as role models for future generations, inspiring young girls to believe in themselves and their dreams.

Empowered women bring a unique perspective and skill set to the workplace. They are confident decision-makers, effective communicators, and collaborative team players. Their contributions lead to increased innovation, productivity, and overall success for their organizations.

Positive, healthy, and authentic relationships are essential for female empowerment. These connections provide women with the love, support, and encouragement they need to thrive. Through healthy boundaries, authentic self-expression, and the dismantling of limiting beliefs, women can embrace their power, confidence, and worthiness of success. As more and more women step into their full potential, we can create a world where all women feel empowered to pursue their dreams and make a meaningful impact on society.

Cultivating positive, healthy, and authentic relationships is a journey of self-discovery and intentional effort. Here are some actionable tips to embark on this path toward empowerment:

1. **Self-Reflection and Identification:** Take time to introspect and identify the qualities you seek in a relationship. What values, interests, and communication styles resonate with you? Recognizing your needs and desires is the first step towards attracting and nurturing fulfilling connections.
2. **Choose Wisely:** Surround yourself with individuals who uplift and inspire you. Seek out friends, partners, and mentors who genuinely care for your well-being, celebrate your successes, and offer constructive support during

challenges. Remember, you have the power to choose the company you keep.
3. **Set Clear Boundaries:** Establishing and maintaining healthy boundaries is crucial for any relationship. Clearly communicate your expectations, limits, and non-negotiables. Remember, saying "no" is a powerful act of self-preservation and self-respect.
4. **Practice Open Communication:** Foster an environment of open and honest communication. Share your thoughts, feelings, and vulnerabilities with trusted individuals. Effective communication builds trust, deepens connection, and allows for authentic self-expression.
5. **Embrace Vulnerability:** Vulnerability is not a weakness but a sign of strength and courage. Allow yourself to be seen and heard for who you truly are. Share your fears, insecurities, and dreams with those who have earned your trust. Vulnerability fosters deeper connections and creates a space for genuine support and understanding.
6. **Cultivate Self-Love:** Self-love is the foundation of any healthy relationship. Treat yourself with kindness, compassion, and respect. Prioritize your own needs and well-being. When you love and value yourself, you attract relationships that mirror that love and respect.
7. **Seek Support:** If you struggle to cultivate positive relationships or feel stuck in unhealthy patterns, seek professional guidance. Therapists and counselors can provide valuable tools and strategies for improving communication, setting boundaries, and developing healthy relationship dynamics.
8. **Join Supportive Communities:** Connect with like-minded women who share your values and aspirations. Join women's groups, online communities, or attend workshops and events focused on female empowerment. Surrounding yourself with a supportive network can foster personal growth, provide valuable insights, and offer encouragement on your journey.
9. **Celebrate Your Achievements:** Acknowledge and celebrate your successes, big or small. Recognize your strengths, talents, and accomplishments. Sharing your joy

and pride with loved ones reinforces your sense of self-worth and empowers you to reach even greater heights.
10. **Practice Gratitude:** Cultivate a daily practice of gratitude. Expressing appreciation for the positive relationships in your life strengthens those bonds and fosters a positive mindset. Gratitude also opens your heart to new connections and opportunities for growth.

Building positive, healthy, authentic relationships takes time and effort. Be patient with yourself and others. Embrace the journey of self-discovery and connection. As you cultivate these empowering relationships, you will unlock your full potential, unleash your confidence, and step into a life filled with joy, purpose, and fulfillment.

Embarking on the journey towards female empowerment often involves finding a supportive sisterhood - a group of women who uplift, inspire, and champion each other's growth. These connections can be pivotal in fostering self-awareness, building confidence, and achieving success. Here's how to find your tribe and cultivate empowering friendships:

1. Explore Online Communities:
    - **Online Forums and Discussion Boards:** Participate in online discussions related to topics you care about. Engage with women who share your passions and challenges.
    - **Virtual Meetups and Events:** Attend virtual events, webinars, and workshops focused on female empowerment. These platforms offer opportunities to connect with like-minded women from around the world.
2. Join Local Organizations and Clubs:
    - **Women's Networking Groups:** Many cities have organizations dedicated to connecting and empowering women in various fields. These groups often host networking events, workshops, and mentoring programs.
    - **Community Centers and Volunteer Organizations:** Volunteering for a cause you care

about is a great way to meet women who share your values and dedication to making a difference.
3. Attend Conferences and Retreats:
    - **Women's Empowerment Conferences:** These events bring together women from diverse backgrounds to share their stories, expertise, and wisdom. Attending conferences can inspire you, expand your network, and introduce you to potential mentors and collaborators.
    - **Wellness and Personal Growth Retreats:** These retreats offer a safe and supportive space for women to connect with themselves and others on a deeper level. You can build meaningful connections and gain valuable insights through workshops, group activities, and shared experiences.
4. Leverage Your Existing Network:
    - **Friends and Family:** Talk to your friends and family about your desire to connect with other women who are passionate about personal growth and empowerment. They may know of groups or individuals who would fit you well.
    - **Colleagues and Mentors:** Reach out to women you admire in your workplace or industry. They may be able to introduce you to their networks or offer valuable advice on finding your sisterhood.
5. Be Open to New Connections:
    - **Strike up Conversations:** Don't be afraid to initiate conversations with women you meet at events, workshops, or in your daily life. A simple "hello" can lead to a meaningful connection.
    - **Attend Social Gatherings:** Accept invitations to social events, even if you don't know many people. It's an opportunity to expand your circle and potentially meet new friends.
6. **Be Authentic:** Show up as your true self. Share your passions, challenges, and dreams. Authenticity attracts genuine connections and fosters a sense of belonging.

Remember, finding your sisterhood is a process of exploration and discovery. Be patient, persistent, and open to new experiences. When you surround yourself with women who uplift and inspire you, you create a powerful network of support that can propel you toward your goals and aspirations.

Incorporating thoughts of self-worth into your daily life is a powerful tool for opening yourself up to success and fulfillment. Remember, self-worth is an ongoing journey of self-discovery and growth. Be patient with yourself, celebrate your progress, and never stop believing in your worthiness of a fulfilling and successful life.

Incorporating self-care into your daily life is crucial for fostering a healthy lifestyle and overall well-being. Here are some practical tips to help you prioritize self-care and create a sustainable routine:

- **Schedule Self-Care:** Make self-care a non-negotiable part of your schedule, just like any other important appointment.
- **Learn to Say No:** Don't overcommit yourself. It's okay to say no to requests that don't align with your priorities or drain your energy.
- **Seek Support:** If you're struggling to prioritize self-care or maintain a healthy lifestyle, don't hesitate to seek support from friends, family, or a therapist.
- **Be Kind to Yourself:** Remember that self-care is not selfish. It's essential for your physical, mental, and emotional well-being. Treat yourself with kindness and compassion.
- **Be Kind to Yourself:** Remember that self-care is not selfish. It's essential for your physical, mental, and emotional well-being. Treat yourself with kindness and compassion.

By incorporating these tips into your daily routine, you'll create a sustainable self-care practice that supports your overall health and well-being. Remember, self-care is a journey, not a destination. Be patient with yourself, celebrate small victories, and continuously explore new ways to nourish your mind, body, and soul.

Integrating self-love into your daily life is fundamental to attracting positive and kind relationships, both personally and professionally. When you value and care for yourself, you naturally radiate an energy that draws others towards you. Here are some actionable tips to cultivate self-love and create a magnetic presence:

- **Pursue Your Passions:** Engage in activities that bring you joy and fulfillment. This helps you connect with your authentic self and radiate positive energy.
- **Practice Mindfulness:** Be present in the moment. Pay attention to your thoughts, feelings, and sensations without judgment. This helps you cultivate self-awareness and develop a deeper connection with yourself.
- **Positive Self-Talk:** Be mindful of your inner dialogue. Challenge negative thoughts and replace them with positive affirmations. Talk to yourself with kindness and compassion.
- **Prioritize Your Needs:** Listen to your body and mind. Take breaks when needed, set boundaries, and say no to things that don't align with your values or goals.
- **Practice Forgiveness:** Forgive yourself for past mistakes and imperfections. Holding onto resentment only hurts you. Let go of the past and embrace the present moment.
- **Celebrate Your Achievements:** Acknowledge and celebrate your successes, big or small. Give yourself credit for your hard work and dedication.
- **Surround Yourself with Positivity:** Spend time with people who uplift and support you. Avoid negative influences that drain your energy or undermine your confidence.

These self-love practices will cultivate a strong sense of self-worth and radiate positive energy by incorporating them into your daily life. This will naturally attract kind and supportive individuals into your personal and professional life, fostering healthy and fulfilling relationships. Remember, self-love is an ongoing journey, not a destination. Be patient with yourself, celebrate your progress, and continue to nurture your inner light.

Self-worth practices profoundly impact your ability to attract success and financial freedom. When you believe in your value and capabilities, you open yourself up to opportunities and make choices that align with your goals. Here are some actionable tips to cultivate self-worth and manifest abundance:

- **Visualize Success:** Spend a few minutes visualizing yourself achieving your financial goals. Imagine the life you desire, the impact you want to make, and the financial freedom you wish to attain.
- **Positive Self-Talk:** Monitor your inner dialogue and challenge any negative thoughts or self-doubt related to money and success. Replace them with empowering affirmations that reinforce your worthiness and capabilities.
- **Invest in Yourself:** Continuously learn and grow by investing in your personal and professional development. Take courses, attend workshops, read books, and network with successful individuals.
- **Celebrate Financial Wins:** Acknowledge and celebrate even small financial victories. This reinforces your progress and motivates you to continue on your path to financial freedom.
- **Set Clear Financial Goals:** Define your financial objectives clearly and create a plan to achieve them. This provides direction and focus for your efforts.
- **Practice Financial Discipline:** Develop a budget, track your spending, and save regularly. Financial discipline empowers you to take control of your financial future.

When you consistently integrate these self-worth practices into your daily routine, you cultivate a strong belief in your abilities and attract the success and financial freedom you desire. Remember, self-worth is a journey of self-discovery and growth. Embrace the process, celebrate your achievements, and never stop believing in your potential to create a life of abundance and fulfillment.

Giving yourself permission to always honor who you are is extremely important when you allow yourself to experience self-care, self-love, and self-worth. Never feel guilty when doing these things for yourself; instead, give yourself permission to enjoy the process. In doing so, you will be able to give more to those around you.

***

To contact Yolanda:

Phone number 1 (702) 766-4599

Website: https://21dayswithyolanda.com

Facebook: https://www.facebook.com/yshoegal

Instagram: https://www.instagram.com/iamyolandamartinez/

LinkedIn: https://www.linkedin.com/in/yolanda-martinez-24606913/

Dr. Jason I. Henderson

Dr. Jason I. Henderson was born in Pocatello, Idaho, the youngest of 9 children. His parents were both teenagers during the depression and raised their family with a great appreciation for frugalness. Since his dad is a veteran of WWII and served overseas for 29 months, he has a keen appreciation and love for this great country.

Having followed the typical "Poor Dad" advice Jason obtained a B.S. degree from Brigham Young University, a Ph.D. from Purdue University, and completed postdoc work at Caltech. He has 28 published peer reviewed scientific papers including 3 articles in *Science* magazine and 5 issued US Patents.

"If you are so smart…why aren't you rich?" was a question posed to and that haunted Jason. Motivated to become wealthy in the most efficient manner, Jason started to do research. Reading numerous books, attending seminars, interviewing successful people and learning from mentors has led to what he deems a systematic way to wealth.

Jason's highest and noblest calling is being a husband and father to 6 children. They are his motivation to do what he does. He wants to leave the world a better place through his children and by helping others to uplevel their financial education through books, speaking engagements and his podcast Master Your Millions.

Understanding the 5 levels of Wealth Creation.

By Dr. Jason I. Henderson

When I was a post-doctoral fellow at the California Institute of Technology, our lab was a collection of some of the brightest and best chemists from around the world. Our group had published an impressive list of scientific papers in the best industry journals, been awarded dozens of patents, and was known for our novel research. To top it off, I worked with a professor who was later awarded the Nobel Prize in Chemistry.

One day we were all discussing a concept on the leading edge of chemistry when he looked at us and said, "if you are so smart, why aren't you rich?" I don't think the question was directed at any one of us in particular, however, I took it straight to heart as though it was aimed directly at me. And that question bothered me - a lot.

After finishing my schooling, I started my first job in the San Francisco Bay area. It was the late 1990s when the biotech and dot-com bubbles were in full swing. Venture capitalists were throwing money at all kinds of propositions and every company that put forward an interesting idea. That abundance of investment capital made it possible for me to have a 6-figure starting salary. I was riding high and feeling like I had really arrived.

Then reality set in. Housing near my office was inflating at an astonishing rate. Most of the professionals I knew, even with both the husband and the wife working high-salaried jobs, struggled to buy a home. The real estate market was climbing at an astonishing rate, and often a house would sell for far more than the asking price, with dozens of bidders driving the cost higher. We were incredibly lucky to get a small home on a decent size lot so our two young sons would have a place to play.

Not only was housing expensive, all other things associated with living in the Bay area were as well. For example, property taxes directly reflected the sales price of a house. Due to the rising market at the time, this resulted in my property taxes being nearly 4 times as much as my neighbor's. Even though our houses were similar in size, he had purchased his house 2 decades earlier when the market was more reasonable. Groceries, gas, and every other normal living expense were so high, it was very difficult to provide for our small family.

After working for a very short time, it became abundantly clear that despite having a Ph.D. and a "high" paying job, we were living paycheck to paycheck. The situation was discouraging, and I began to feel like the American dream had been annihilated.

To me, the American Dream was all about your children doing better than you. With my current standard of living, that did not seem like even a remote possibility. And my professor's question continued to haunt me, "If you are so smart, why aren't you rich?"

When I started my college education I didn't know much about chemistry, yet at the end of my Ph.D. research, I was a world expert in my field. There was one thing I was confident of; I knew how to learn. I knew I could approach any problem and within a short time find solutions.

With this confidence, I set out to discover the secrets of becoming wealthy. I read books like *Think and Grow Rich*, *The Richest Man in Babylon*, *Rich Dad Poor Dad*, and numerous other books on the subject. I studied biographies of some of America's wealthiest people and families. I talked to people who had been successful at achieving financial freedom. What I discovered is that there are essentially 5 levels of wealth which build on each other, and when you learn to master one level and implement the characteristics of the next level, you naturally progress from level to level.

Level 1: Dependence/Poverty.

We all come into this world at this lowest level. Regardless of how wealthy our family is, when we are born, we are 100% dependent on someone else to provide and care for us. As we grow older, we begin to have a choice to stay at the dependence level or advance toward the next level.

Poverty is very similar to dependence in that, since we have no resources to speak of, we are dependent on others – government, family, friends, benefactors etc. Poverty though, is more than simply a lack of monetary resources; it's a state of existence that permeates every aspect of life. It's not simply about having no money coming in or going out; it's about a mindset and a set of circumstances that can trap individuals in a seemingly unbreakable cycle.

I found that in general those choosing to live in poverty have the following characteristics:

1. Self-centered focus. Many people a total focused on themselves. The focus on mere survival prevents the ability to look beyond oneself, limiting potential engagement with others and the community
2. Financial stagnation. Without money flowing in or out, opportunities for growth and development are stunted.
3. Health struggles. Poor health often accompanies poverty as quality healthcare and nutrition are typically out of reach.
4. External discipline. Living under constant supervision or control by others, such as government assistance programs or charitable organizations, takes away personal autonomy and self-respect.

Poverty's influence extends deep into the psyche, dampening hope and aspirations, lessening confidence, and affecting a person's perception of his/her value and worth. It's not just a financial condition, but an existential one. The mindset can become one of scarcity and limitation, where dreams are deferred, and ambitions are smothered.

Social implications of being in poverty often include isolation and stigmatization. Lack of resources limits access to education, healthcare, and even basic social interactions. It creates a barrier that can divide families and communities.

The question then arises, what is the pathway or mechanism to get beyond the poverty level?

Plain and simple, the solution is: WORK. Yes, the critical step in getting out of poverty is employment. A job isn't just about earning money; it's about dignity, purpose and a sense of belonging. It's about taking control of one's life and beginning the journey towards financial independence.

You must bear in mind; poverty isn't a life sentence – it's only the starting point! With the right support, mindset and opportunities, individuals can rise above their circumstances and embark on a journey towards financial stability and personal fulfillment.

Let me say it again, work is the key to progressing beyond dependence and poverty to the next level.

Level 2 – Survival.

The second level, Survival, is a slight improvement over dependence and poverty. There is still little income, however, your financial life is still precarious and fraught with uncertainty. This is where I was in San Franciso. The survival level is a world of living paycheck to paycheck, where financial emergencies can lead to disaster and dreams seem out of reach.

Like the previous level, I discovered that people on this level generally have several characteristics in common.

1. Constant struggle. You must get up and go to work, so the rent can be paid, the car payment made, insurance, food, and on and on. The stress of making ends meet can be overwhelming, leading to both mental and physical exhaustion.
2. Debt burden. When living from paycheck to paycheck, often unexpected expenses can be hug. To cope with those expenses, often consumer debt is employed to get by. Yet, consumer debt should be considered bad debt. When this kind of debt is employed, the common plight is minimal credit card payments giving rise to a heavy weight that can feel inescapable.
3. Lack of future planning. Without savings, emergency funds or retirement plans, the future can feel bleak and uncontrollable. People start to believe things will never get better. I certainly did. I was going to work until I dropped dead – and possibly be in debt when I did. In short, a better future seemed unrealistic and out of reach. That is precisely why most people stop thinking about the future.
4. External discipline. Like the poverty level, individuals in survival mode are still largely controlled by external forces such as employers and creditors. They are told when to come to work, where to work, what to do at work and when they can go home. The credit card bill and other bills are due,

regardless of how you feel or whether you have enough money.

All these factors certainly have a psychological impact. The constant pressure of survival can lead to anxiety, depression and other mental health challenges.

The feeling of always being one step away from disaster can erode confidence and lead to a sense of hopelessness and frustration. Individuals at this level often feel as though no matter how hard they work, they will never get anywhere.

What are the most typical strategies people employ to help themselves move forward from the survival level?

1. Budgeting. Learning to live within one's means and cutting unnecessary expenses can create breathing room.
2. Debt management. Creating a plan to tackle debt can lead to a sense of control and progress.
3. Seeking support. Community programs, financial counseling, mentors, and supportive networks can help.

These three have one thing in common, which is the key to going beyond the survival level: SAVINGS.

Consistently putting something away – even a small amount – creates peace of mind, a safety net, and new possibilities. With determination, planning and support, it's possible to move beyond mere survival and into a life of greater stability and promise.

Like the last level, the survival level is not a destination, but a passage. With determination, planning and support, it's possible to move beyond mere survival and into a life of greater stability and promise.

Using the words of George S. Clason: "A portion of everything you make is yours to keep." (Hint add the work "forever" to the end of that quote and you will have found a profound accelerant to higher levels.

Level 3 – Comfort.

This level, though higher than the first two, is dangerous, since comfort and ease can give the illusion of security. This level is marked by stability, but also usually by complacency. Here, while it may seem like a welcome respite from the struggles of survival, it can also be a trap that prevents further growth.

You don't want to stagnate at this level. How do you know you are on the Comfort level?

1. Dependency on a W-2 job, or in other words, an employer to provide income and savings. A reliance on regular employment with a semblance of steady, predictable income can give individuals a false sense of security and, as a result, make them vulnerable to economic shifts and unexpected events. Dependence on an employer for retirement and savings plans can limit control and options.
2. Individuals at this level have enough money to enjoy a few luxuries and often enjoy the feeling of "arrival" they get by purchasing expensive showy items, such as a new car, a large home and possibly the occasional vacation. These items come at the expense of build lasting wealth.
3. High risk investments and liabilities. People on this level often look for quick ways to wealth, putting themselves at a lot of risk before having a substantial foundation of saving and proper insurance. Often the culprit is the lack of proper financial education. Without it individuals may jeopardize their financial health with this types of behavior.
4. Continued external discipline. Despite increased stability, the comfort level still includes being disciplined by others such as landlords or employers, reflecting the lack of full financial autonomy.

The tell-tale signs of being in the comfort level is often a lack of motivation and a tendency to settle for the status quo. The very stability that defines this level can become a barrier to further growth and exploration. In order to avoid this trap and progress, financial education is critical at this stage. Understanding how money works, why we actually have banks and the difference between, and asset and a liability growth can unlock the door to prosperity.

Maybe you can see the way beyond the comfort level. The reality is most cannot. The key to moving on to the next level is: OWNERSHIP.

Transitioning to the next level involves owning income generating assets. You can no longer trade your time for money. There will come a time when you are no longer able to make that trade and even when you have diligently saved, it will not be enough. Think about it, can you save 10% of your income for 40 years and then live for the next 40 years on solely what you have saved? You much crack the code of having money work for you. Money at work, works 24/7/365. Whether it's real estate, stocks, small businesses, or assets such as whole life insurance, owning these assets can provide passive income and greater financial flexibility. The plateau of Comfort is a significant milestone, but it should not be the end of the journey. With awareness, education and ambition, individuals can transcend comfort and reach the next level.

Level 4 - Prosperity.

Prosperity is where individuals begin to see the fruits of their labors and make significant strides towards financial independence. It's a stage characterized by wise investments, passive income and personal growth.

How do you recognize someone who is living on the Prosperity level?

1. Self-discipline. This is the first level where you are disciplined more by yourself than by external forces. The shift from external to internal discipline reflects a newfound control and responsibility over one's financial destiny.
2. Understanding of, and investing in assets, not the purchase of liabilities. Building a diverse portfolio of income generating assets, especially those that produce passive income, is central to this stage of wealth development.
3. Significant financial reserves. Savings for emergencies, retirement and enjoyment provide stability. No longer is the car breaking down or a health emergency as catastrophic as it is on the other levels we have discussed.
4. Time for personal growth. With financial security comes the opportunity to invest in oneself through education, hobbies and personal development.

Prosperity brings a sense of accomplishment and the confidence to explore new opportunities. It fosters a growth mindset and a broader perspective on life. Yet this level is not the end level, there is more.

What is the key to advancing to the next and highest level? CONTROL

In order to reach the next level you must begin to control your own financial situation. You must be largely in control of your money, your time, and your health. People at the Prosperity level must be very careful to surround themselves with like-minded individuals and continue their self-development with mentors and coaches.

Level 5 – Abundance/Wealth

Level 5 is all about freedom. Time and money freedom allows you the opportunity to increase your impact and legacy. It's the stage where financial considerations transform into broader life philosophies. The abundance level brings a shift in perspective from self to others. Wealth becomes a tool for impact, whether through philanthropy, mentorship or community engagement.

How do you know you have reached level 5?

1. Uninterrupted compound interest based on key financial strategies like the Infinite Banking Concept.
2. Passive income greater than expenses. Ideally you are earning more while you sleep than while you are awake. Mastery over financial instruments and investments provides continuous income growth, whether you work today or not.
3. Freedom to choose what you do, when you do it, how, how often and with whom represents the ultimate control over one's life.
4. Building generational wealth. The shift to thinking of others naturally leads to planning for future generations. This is a direct reflection of a long-term perspective and a sense of stewardship. Legacy becomes much more than simply money left to heirs. You start to realize it is not what to leave to someone it is what you live in them.
5. Continued investment in knowledge and growth. Since you are at a higher level does not mean you stagnate. You seek

further learning through masterminds, seminars and mentorship. You start to want to be a teacher and mentor to others.
6. The ability to discipline others, whether employees or tenants, signifies a transition from being a player to being a coach in the financial game.
7. Philanthropy and social impact using wealth to make a positive difference in the world can be both rewarding and influential.

When you arrive at this level is the journey over? While a legacy of wealth and abundance might be considered the ultimate culmination of a financial journey, it can also be a beginning. It opens doors to new adventures, challenges and opportunities to leave a lasting mark on the world.

Basically, what I have discovered is the passage through the five levels of wealth is a complex and multifaceted one filled with toil, pain, frustration as well as gratitude, impact and cause.

Remember, this journey is not merely about money; it's also about freedom, personal growth, societal impact, and ultimately the legacy one leaves behind. It's not so much what you leave to someone, it's what you leave in them. From the depths of poverty to the heights of abundance, the path is filled with lessons, challenges and triumphs, each contributing to a richer understanding of what it means to truly be wealthy.

***

To contact Jason:

Dr J, as he is affectionately called can be best reached at:

www.askjasonh.com

InstaGram @jasonihenderson on Instagram

Facebook: https://www.facebook.com/hendersonandfloyd

Master Your Millions (https://masteryourmillionspodcast.com/) can be heard on all podcast platforms.

Ken 'Dr. Smiley' Rochon, Jr., PhD

Ken 'Dr. Smiley' Rochon, Jr., PhD is a renaissance man, humanitarian, and an accomplished serial entrepreneur. He is a social proof celebrity event photographer, international keynote speaker, and published author of 60 books.

Amplifluence.com is his new company helping Authors & Speakers monetize their influence and amplify their positive impact in the media.

TheUmbrellaSyndicate.com (a Marketing, Promotion, & Media Company); PerfectPublishing.com (a Book Publishing Company) and his radio show 'Dr. Smiley Show…Amplifying HOPE' on Voice America Influencer Channel is a platform he uses to discuss building community, fatherhood, leadership, success principles, and values.

Ken, who lost his mother to Alzheimer's complications, desires to live a life of purpose where he leaves a legacy of love for his son to model. He is the Co-Founder of the non-profit organization TheKeepSmilingMovement.com. He has published over 200 books of leaders. The movement shares these books with everyone needing a 'D.O.S.E. of HOPE.'

His love of the arts and sciences inspired him to travel to over 100 countries. His favorite place to be is with his son K3, the light of his life.

The Evolution of Dr. Smiley

By Ken 'Dr. Smiley' Rochon, Jr., PhD

$72,000… that is what it would be worth to reach 20 million people. Do you want to reach 20 million people with your message? I know I do!

Reading my chapter may be the best decision you make today, as I intend to offer you $36,000 in value with no strings attached. Why? Because an author on a purpose driven life is not motivated by anything more than impact. So, if my chapter allows us to connect and share your story, then it will be a triumph and a compelling reason for adding my voice to this anthology.

When I was born over fifty years ago, I had no idea who 'Dr. Smiley' was, nor did I have any inclination of who he would become to me.

I was born in Warwick, Rhode Island, and whisked away to Paris, France, as an Army brat. Twelve years and twelve countries later, I was back in Rhode Island trying to figure out how to use a phone. After devoting my life to soccer and believing this would be my life, I was depressed and disappointed that the return to America would be void of my biggest passion… Soccer. Pele was my role model, and he could not prepare me for the life I would lead in a small farm town in Galesburg, Illinois. This town was so isolated, that I was accused of being a 'Nazi Nigger Lover' because I came from Germany and was unaware that discrimination was a way of life in this town. The school was integrated, but the real estate told a different story. If you were on this side of the tracks, you were white, and the other side was predominantly black.

The reason I share this part of my life was that my dad and mom never taught me about discrimination or that it even existed. Near the end of my mother's life, her last thoughts as a victim of Alzheimer's were to support Native Americans and expose the atrocities of the White Man on this beautiful culture and race. Mind you, my mom is white, married to a white man.

I always wanted to be an author and more importantly to matter in the world. I defined being an author as someone who was credible and worthy of attention and merit. Over thirty years of believing this never caused me to even write one sentence in a book... until I was a caregiver for my mom. That was the catalyst to stepping into my power---one born of a fear that I would die before I ever did anything to make a difference. I am not sure if all humans feel this way, but I certainly knew I could not be a person that failed to leave a legacy. I had to write a book.

This ignited action and a book went to print thirteen months after my mom passed. It was titled 'Becoming the Perfect Networker... Succeeding 1 Connection @ a Time'.

This was a financial disaster, and any sane person would have written off the $22,000 loss as an act of ignorance. But a prayer to God helped me understand this was a message that most authors experience---perhaps a smaller financial loss, perhaps larger. Most quit with this impossible challenge to get a return on the investment (save the return on the effort). I would have quit, too, but God was clear... this was a lesson on how messed up self-publishing could be for a new author.

God and my mom were teaching me my most valuable lesson... a Legacy is earned with an unstoppable attitude. I invested another $3000 to republish and reprint this grammatically incorrect nightmare. It was grammatically incorrect because of hiring a college professor in Florida that obviously did not have a clue about editing or writing. He fleeced me for over $1000, and a lesson was learned that without social proof, testimonials, and vetting, you are positioning yourself as a lamb ready to be fleeced or slaughtered of any dreams you will chase in the future.

Perfect Publishing was born because of this nightmare. My valuable lesson created a much-needed company to protect future authors from bad decisions. I learned quickly how many leaders would love to write their book but just didn't understand how to complete it. How could I help more people step into their power to become an author, an inspiration, and a legacy for the people they loved? I needed to go back to the drawing board and find out where the pitfalls are that stop people.

The first pitfall was being inspired enough to even do the book / project. Many leaders just didn't know if they were worthy of being Authors. Many thought 'I need to accomplish more before I can write this book', or 'I need more money, success, or perfection in my life'. Not knowing the gifts they had to share with the world already existed in their hearts and minds.

My focus became on how to overcome this challenge. I figured it out with some very simple out of the box techniques that caused almost 100% of my writers to become authors. It was about inspiration and breaking down the project into bite size weekly portions. Typically, a leader was able to complete this process in 3 to 6 months when I finally understood the dynamics of what would motivate them to compete, complete, and lunge into the finish line of a new identity as an author.

The second issue became very clear to me that moving a book required a marketing approach and system---one fueled by social proof and testimonials. This was another gap that was causing the authors' great frustration. Most authors (almost 99%) were writing their first book, and the sales were so low that there just wasn't a desire to write another book. "Why would I write another book after I just wrote my best book… that took my life to create?" This was the question that was either internally plaguing them or that was shared with me with despair and disgust.

It was evident that there must be an approach or sequence that is causing this demise of the author's impact. It quickly cleared up when I looked up their Amazon book listing and their social media. It was as if they believed that the book being delivered from their hearts and minds would magically awaken the world or through some osmosis would get into their avatars' being. I later termed this the Doctor Delivering the Baby (book) methodology. Basically, when the book is printed, magically the world will find out about this birth.

Consider this formula and you will be enlightened at the mystery of failure (no desire to write another book and loss again).

$$c \times D = I$$

'C' is content and although it is critical and necessary, it proportionally has so little bearing on the 'I' which represents 'Impact and/or Income, and/or Inspiration'. The missing variable for having your 'I' result be impressive enough that you wish to do it again, is the arduous, and strategic marathon of a marketing campaign (typically a year or two long) is the Big 'D' for Distribution. The 'D' is the energy and fuel you need to keep content alive. Just like feeding a baby every day, you feed your book the marketing attention it needs and inevitably a tipping point much like Malcolm Gladwell describes in his book with the same title will result in the proportion you are consistent with your branding and messaging.

As I have studied this insane perspective that the world is awaiting your book (unless you are an influencer with an enormous following), there is no one who knows your book exists... save the family you shared this dream with and your friends that will out of obligation buy your book for $20 with almost no intention of consuming, sharing, or being impacted by your brilliance. Because your friends know you, they have a difficult time adjusting to see you be bigger than how they define you in their lives.

This challenge is universal. Hence the reason when you make it big, your friends show up sharing they know you. ☺ Unless your friends have influence, I have learned it is best to show up as an unknown and create an identity you wish to be taken seriously for being. I recently became 'Dr. Smiley'. This was welcomed in the new world. But it just could not be taken seriously by my family... well, my son loves the name and probably overstates my fame at this point. But having a young son to motivate you to be his hero is a gift in and of itself.

What I have learned is that I was almost 99% incorrect in how much proportion of my resources (money and time) should be spent on making my book versus moving my book. It turns out that if you spend three months or even one year writing your book, you are only doing what an Olympic athlete would do to get to the starting line of his/her performance or race. In other words, if you only wrote a book and thought that all the writing was the win, you would be thinking that all your workouts to qualify to be in the Olympics should be a medal earned. You have earned almost nothing by printing your book. I don't say this to be cruel or dissuade you from a wonderful accomplishment for your immediate family and friends. I am only putting this in perspective that there are over 7 billion people on this planet. What percentage are you impacting, inspiring, and causing to be fans of your passion and purpose?

My goal when I complete a book is never to stop marketing or printing it. That changes the book accomplishment to almost 1% of the work. I spend about 99% of my resources (money and time) making sure the book has an impact. The closer I am able to be to 99%, the closer I have found the book impacts the world instead of only qualifying to compete to qualify to be at the Olympics. ☺

My final awakening of publishing is the misconception of moving a book versus creating abundance. A book is not just a delivery project to your family or even the world; it is hopefully a means of positioning you to be a solution, a leader, an expert, a sought-after sage of your domain. My book 'Becoming the Perfect Networker… Succeeding 1 Connection @ a Time' positioned me as 'The Man Who Wrote the Book on Networking'. I was on over 50 podcasts, and I became relevant to people who were just going to networking events and collecting cards.

In 2015, I met a man whom I lovingly refer to as a 'Prophet of Joy'. His name is Barry Shore. He simply handed me a card with 'KEEP SMILING' as the two words that would awaken my soul. I couldn't stop thinking about how congruent this message was to my mom's ability to bring positivity to my life, my family, her students, and her friends.

I shared with Barry that this card had awakened my soul, and I believe after his responses to what he is doing with the card, that I could create a movement. Little did he know that day that the card would be photographed thousands of times with amazing authors, business entrepreneurs, leaders, models, musicians, speakers, and anyone sporting a beautiful smile (teeth or not).

With all these photos taken, it was an easy decision to see what would happen if I created and published a little 6 x 6 book with all these amazing smiles and chose one of the leaders to share their story. We have almost 200 of these thematic books on Amazon and on our website (www.theKEEPSMILINGmovement.com) for FREE. The mission is to help save lives through dental and mental wellness. The book 'The Science of Smiles' was released to share the importance of Smiles as part of your daily nutrition for your soul.

I've found my best strategy for making a difference in the world... keep writing and keep giving my books away to people who need a solution to something I have written about. I average giving over 1 thousand books away a year (pre-pandemic) and over 10 thousand books a year as eBooks. If your book inspires someone to be better or awakens them to focus on you as a solution to their happiness, I assure you life will be better for both of you.

Before the 2020 pandemic, my son (Kenny Rochon, III, aka K3) was not an author. He now has 14 books by his eleventh birthday. He currently has over 150 five-star reviews for all his books because he understands at age 11 how to convert sales into testimonials and reinvest his profits proportionally into future books.

It was also the year I started my dissertation through the International University of Entreprenology with a PhD in Philosophy. This gave rise to a new way of being identified... 'Dr. Smiley'. I come from a family of high learners, so this was a prestigious advance on my degrees, but my true motivations were to make my mom proud, and for my son to see when the chips are down, you can still come out on top if you want this enough.

We soon discussed the possibility of him being an author before his 7th birthday. He was open to this as it was a book entitled 'Kenny's Favorite Jokes'. He even had a page with some of his originals which will remain my favorite forever.

When the book was delivered to him on his 6th birthday, he was concerned with only one thing... is it on Amazon and could I prove it. The delivery of this beautiful color book created only about 1% of the excitement he expressed when he did indeed see his book and name on Amazon.com. This was one of my proudest moments as a father.

He has since arranged, googled, searched, and put together 'Kenny's Favorite Riddles', 'Kenny's Favorite Science Facts', 'Kenny's Favorite Things to Know' and 'Kenny's Favorite Trivia'. He is finally paying tribute to his birthday theme of patriotism with his newest book 'Kenny's Favorite Places in America' Something I show anyone with interest in my son's accomplishments is a photo of a letter he is proudly holding from President Biden. Kenny has proven that the distribution and continuous book festivals, marketing, podcasting, social media, videos, and writing more books is creating the 'Tipping Point' mentioned earlier.

His success led him to observe that if he wrote 4 more books by his 10th birthday, he would have a book for every year he is alive. He surpassed this goal with his 12th book 'My First 10 Years... Philosophies for Living a Better Life & World.' This book shares all his knowledge he has gleaned from writing eleven books and how he has matured as a communicator and thinker.

To return to my opening sentence... '$72,000... that is what it would be worth to reach 20 million people. Do you want to reach 20 million people with your message?' I do. This is my mark and largest project of my life thus far. I intend to honor great inspiring leaders with a 'Chicken Soup meets TED Talk' formula for inspiring HOPE in the world. The project is titled 'D.O.S.E. of HOPE' and the acronym stands for the amazing chemicals God has created that are released when we feel alive and have 'HOPE' (Dopamine, Oxytocin, Serotonin, and Endorphins).

I decided to research the impact of asking the question 'Who Am I?' and 'How did I create my Who?'. Turns out the more we commit, devote, and invest (as referenced in Malcolm Gladwell's book 'Outliers'), the more we will create a 'Who' we love. This relationship to our love of ourselves allows us to create an equally powerful 'Why' otherwise known as a 'Purpose'. The higher the variable of 'Purpose' we claim as it relates to the needs of humanity, the higher our 'How' will be (also known as your 'Impact' in the world).

So, the variables can be shown as:

$$Y \times W \times H = Sph$$

('Y' = You; 'W' = Why / Purpose; 'H' = How / Impact and 'Sph' = Smiles per Hour)

This is a TED talk in the making that I believe will even impress Simon Sinek. Our happiness is best derived from our ability to bring happiness to others and the world. The close second ingredient I work tirelessly to teach my son is the gratitude reflection time needed for us to have the capacity to understand that our power to impact the world is fueled by our gratitude for being alive.

A friend recently gave me a wonderful acronym for H.O.P.E. ... 'Hold On Pain Ends'. This inspired a book to honor my mentor Barry Shore, aka 'The Ambassador of Joy' and my co-founder of the KEEP SMILING movement to publish our first book together... 'A Pocket Full of Acronyms'.

Every book I have mentioned in this chapter and the other 33 or so are all available for FREE because I believe a book is a business card with a big message designed to create conversations, opportunities, and legacy. Simply Kennect with me, and any and all of the ebooks are available for asking.

My mom had an expression 'Look for the Good in People and You Will Always Find It'. I thank my mom every day I am alive to know that the world has good people worth amplifying their goodness... which is on over 4 million 'KEEP SMILING' cards that have been distributed to people who give the biggest gift that shows their soul at the highest frequency... a SMILE ☺

***

To contact Ken:

Ken 'Dr. Smiley' Rochon, Jr., PhD

Author • Father • Speaker • World Traveler

(C) 202.701.0911

BookDr.Smiley@gmail.com

IG @BookDr.Smiley

https://www.perfectpublishing.com

Manny Lopez

Manny helps create & enhance speakers, coaches, authors, & consultants with strategic PR opportunities & dynamic systems of automation. A husband and father of 3, he devotes his time to creating a lifestyle of being #TooBlessedToBeStressed while creating opportunities for his network of over 30,000 business professionals worldwide!

Currently, he is a paid consultant on lead generation to over 1000 brands worldwide! Featured by INC. Magazine, Manny's work has been showcased on NBC, The Huffington Post, Bloomberg Radio, recently named "BEST NEW MEDIA" at Living Legends at Carnegie Hall, a CEO Space International graduate, and within just 2 years of starting his business, Manny was named "One of the Best" by Facebook when they hit 1 million advertisers!

Today, he uses his skills in building systems & brands to fund his passion project, "From Orphan To CEO" where Manny teaches MENTORSHIP, ENTREPRENEURSHIP, & FAITH to "DAY 1" entrepreneurs, at-risk youth & kids that age out of foster care using his revolutionary award-winning personal development platform, the MANNYfestation: SCHOOL OF BUSINESS! Currently the platform is active in 80+ countries worldwide, translates to 25+ languages, with 30,000+ global users and growing daily!

2 out of 3 kids that age out of foster care, within 1 year, end up DEAD, HOMELESS, or in JAIL! Manny hopes to see 2 out of 3 of these kids have MENTOR, understand ENTREPRENEURSHIP, & own their BUSINESS!

"Dear Me"

By Manny Lopez

I would've liked to start this letter with "hoping this would find you well," but I know it doesn't. You have just found out the opportunity you've worked years for is completely unattainable, and you are absolutely devastated.

How do I know this? Well, to put it bluntly... I'm you. 15 years later.

I'm writing you this letter to give you a perspective on your future. The initial task I gave myself was to give you a warning of things to come. A premonition, if you will, of understanding the path that lies before you.

You've decided to become an entrepreneur! Today is day 1.

Putting the pieces together of your life story was an interesting undertaking that has woven a web of experiences, emotions, & tragedies that has created the man I am today.

I'm still not sure how this letter will conclude as I type these words from my computer desk. I sit here conflicted. Do I help you avoid the upcoming pitfalls you will inevitably face or do I help you instill the confidence to endure the pain of the upcoming years ahead.

With pain comes change. Sometimes we must endure the pain of chaotic blessings to create what embodies the human spirit we become. I truly do believe that.

Maybe this letter simply proves the mantra I live by: "too blessed to be stressed"

Regardless of the adversity, I can look at countless blessings I experience that billions of people on this planet can only dream of. The little things in life we constantly take for granted.

Right now that's probably the furthest from your mind. You are 22 and your wife is pregnant with your 2nd son, you are completely clueless to what your future holds, the ideal life plan you had all mapped out has been shattered to pieces and now you are left facing an unclear path of uncertainty. All you know is that you are done building someone else's dream. It's time to build your own.

But what dream is that? What do you ultimately want to do? What do you become? Are you happy? Are you successful? Do you check off the list you ultimately give Nancy when you begin this journey full time? So many questions, but luckily for you, I'm here to give you some of those answers.

Imagine being able to fast forward over a decade into an idea to see it to fruition. Does it become what you've imagined? Did you make the right decisions along the way?

If I were to do it all over again, how much would I want to change? Would I want to change anything at all? Does everything truly happen for a reason? These questions are what I really want you to ponder. I'm going to give you a glimpse into the life you've created for yourself. What your family dynamic looks like. How things have changed. The dumb decisions you've made along the way and some of the good ideas you've implemented, too.

By the end of this letter, I hope to give you my definitive answer on whether I'd like for you to use this information I'm giving you to forge a new path for yourself or should you keep everything the same. I guess that answer is truly up to you.

Every time I look back on a tragedy I've faced or experienced, when I take a couple years to see how that has impacted my life, I can always seem to find a way to bring it to an understanding of why it was meant to be.

Navigating through life's chaos brought me to my queen. Every turn was pulling me just in the right direction so our paths would meet. The trouble in school that made me switch to the school she attended. The lack of motivation in school that led me to fail that class I had to go to night classes for. The place you first saw her took years of chaotic blessings to make that experience a reality.

Is every major life blessing also connected to a web of chaotic blessings? The farther I look back, the more the reality sinks in that it does.

For instance, over the next 2 years from the day you receive this letter you embark on a journey to discover what kind of business you will create. You will fail many times, becoming homeless twice within that two-year span. What happens within those 2 years really wakes you up to the reality of what is on your shoulders. I can give you many ways you could fix these issues and maybe you will never become homeless at all, but the drive, will, and determination you now have within you because of what you endured cannot be taught. You can't just read a book and now have it. It's a pain you have to feel so you never want to feel it again. It becomes a driving force that leads you to carve out the road ahead.

It's like a video game. One of those RPG types where the character can get stronger as the game progresses. Going through life experiences builds a sense of strength and endurance that only comes by playing the game.

Manny, you've got to play the game!

But just like with video games, there are ways to make the game a little easier to play. Make it easier to win. You can learn from people who have played the game before. You can go directly to the source. That's what I hope this letter can become for you; a way to understand the journey without waiting years to understand the lessons.

You may think all is lost right now but look at how far you've already come from that goofy little adopted kid working at McDeez. You married your high-school sweetheart, now expecting your 2nd son, you've got the experience of at least 10 different industries from the places you've worked at over the years, supported your little family on your own since you were 19, & a present father.

Over the next 15 years, you accomplish a lot. You check off everything on your list you give to Nancy after you became homeless for the 2nd time.

You give her this list in a room that was made from a converted garage. This is currently your home. I'll spare you the details of how you ended up here, but you are about 2 years into this decision to become an entrepreneur. It has not been an easy road.

Imagine you jumped off a cliff without a parachute and you're trying to build one on the way down. Ya, it's kinda like that. You've already been homeless once, you just moved into this garage that's now a 1-bedroom for your family of 4, and you can see the lack of hope in your wife's eyes as she is sitting beside you waiting for you to show up as the man you promised her you would be. Someone she can count on to take care of our little family.

You've lost everything: your home, your car, and your savings. Things just don't seem like they're getting any better and just when you thought things were looking up, you're dealt another blow that leaves you with a decision to make... another *chaotic blessing*, if you will.

It's time for you to take the reins and jump into this entrepreneurship thing full time. You sit Nancy down and give her the 6-year roadmap. You're 24. By 30, you will accomplish 5 things:

1. Move to Lake Elsinore (currently living in OC)
2. Live in a 2-story home (currently living in a garage)
3. Have our daughter (only 2 boys so far)
4. Create a successful business (currently no business)
5. Never be homeless again

I'm happy to say that by 30, you will have checked off everything on this list. I'm writing this letter to you from our 2-story home in Lake Elsinore. Our daughter, Ava, is sleeping next to me just a few feet away. I'm now 37 and we haven't been homeless since we made that promise. I'm a paid consultant to over 1000 brands worldwide, an award-winning entrepreneur, 2x #1 best-selling author, speaker, and I created a program to help foster kids find mentors to start their own businesses! We even turned it into a TV show!

I think you'd be quite happy to see what has become of your ideas. Would there be things I'd change? Probably. Would I still have the life I have today if I did? I'm not sure.

Our life today has its ups and downs. Nothing is ever perfect. I don't expect it to be, but at 37, I've experienced a lot of life I've been privileged to learn from. You're reading this letter at 22. You will find as the years go on, the important things in life become the memories you've created with the people you love. Your kids, your wife, your family.

The balance between work and family is probably your biggest hurdle. You get this obsession with new ideas to see them to fruition.

You've created success before, so everything becomes possible. Hobbies become passion projects. Ideas become brands. Processes become success stories. Sometimes that takes a toll on those around you. Those you don't notice when ideas are becoming reality.

The challenges of being a man who prides himself on having the answers will put a lot of weight on your shoulders. A weight that becomes a responsibility. A responsibility that becomes your life's mission. There are times when the tasks become unbearable, and you tend to shut down. The days become dark as you look to find the motivation that drives you forward. Falling into complacency is your #1 obstacle.

Put God first. Keep your word. Under promise, over deliver. Make weekly date night a priority. Learn the 5 love languages. Forgive. Teach your kids everything you wish you were taught growing up. Capture all the memories. Experience new and exciting things as many times as you can. Serve first. Be a sponge for knowledge. Learn from & collaborate with the people who are influential in the market you want to reach. Do things with purpose. Set the example you want your kids to follow. Always remember, you're too blessed to be stressed.

If I could simplify the qualities I admire & wish to expand upon as I grow older, these would be it. The way I see it, the only way to truly accomplish success in life is not to focus on getting rich. I know a lot of people with money, but no family left to share it with. They live lonely, depressing lives, yearning for the years lost to chasing the dollar.

Chase life. Chase love. Chase memories.

My first priority is to make sure my family has food on the table, but I also want to be at that table sitting with them. I want to know my children. Let my children see what a loving marriage can be. For my sons and daughter to see the love their father has for their mother. To look at it and say "I want a love like that for me one day."

I know I'm not perfect. I fight demons every day that try to torment my happiness; to drive me into thoughts of despair and shame. It won't be easy. There will be days when you won't see any hope for the future. Days filled with an empty shell of the man you thought you'd become. You will face tragedies and losses that will look like impossible mountains to climb… but you will climb them. You will conquer every goal you set out to accomplish. There will be times where you outshine even your own expectations.

Your children will impress you with skills you only dreamed you had within you. It will light up your world to see the passion your family has for the lives they've dreamt for themselves.

Be excited in the uncertainty, for it is in these times that your most precious and most powerful ideas unfold.

Embrace the chaotic blessings. Live knowing that your understanding does not come simultaneously with the lesson… and that's ok.

You're too blessed to be stressed, remember? ;)

Manny

***

To contact Manny:

www.MANNYfestation.com

Jennifer Jehl

I'm a passionate advocate for personal transformation and the power of rediscovering one's true self. After hitting a toxic people-pleasing rock bottom filled with trauma, I embarked on a journey of self-discovery, uncovering my purpose, vision, beliefs, and unshakable confidence.

Today, I walk with authenticity, boundaries, clarity, and direction, driven by a deep desire to serve others. With a specific focus on men's empowerment, my work centers around helping men reignite their passion and reclaim their confidence. I believe in the importance of nurturing the concept of biblical masculinity, recognizing its scarce yet essential role in today's emasculated society.

My comprehensive approach encompasses all aspects of a balanced life, plus my ten traits of biblical masculinity. Through my coaching and mentoring, I guide men to find equilibrium in all the key areas of life. By addressing these vital areas and balancing personal growth with timeless principles - I help empower men to lead lives of fulfillment, purpose, success, and joy.

Run to Your Self

By Jennifer Jehl

"RUN!!!!!!!" My body screamed at me. Nausea and churning made me keel over in pain. I prayed to God that he'd change his mind and that something would happen to make him not show. He had already waved some red flags, and my gut and brain desperately tried to plead with my kind heart. I just chose not to listen, even though I knew it would ruin me.

So he came and quickly started the repetitive cycle of tearing me down to build me back up... rinse and repeat. I justified it all: I deserved it, he didn't mean it, I could change the way he sees me... after all, this was an actor I'd had a crush on since high school.

Our weekends together became more frequent. I traveled to see him more often than he offered the same. I didn't get it since I was a single mom of 3 kids, but I made it happen. The red flags intensified. I became an embarrassment to him; he belittled, yelled, and cursed at me. Soon enough, I was convinced to put an abhorrent amount of money into a "real estate investment business," quickly noticing that I was funding his whole life. He started to become angry with me when I left his city to return home. I started to realize that it was because he couldn't maintain control of me when I left.

After almost two years of long-distance weekends with high highs and low lows, I made the ultimate toxic move. I convinced my family that the best thing was to move to his state. I took my three kids out of their school district and dragged my parents along too. I eliminated things that "wouldn't fit" in our life together.

Two weeks in, he hurt me for the first time. Soon, the jaw grabs against the wall turned into bruises that covered my scalp. Terrified, I was convinced it was my fault. He made me dependent on him, and I fought for his approval.

Then, he started being verbally abusive to my son, Donie, who was five at the time. Donie has special needs in the form of complex cardiac defects and developmental delays. He'd already survived so many surgeries at this point. How could I let someone talk down to him? WHAT have I done? I started to realize that this man was full of insecurity, and I got angry. I was living in HELL. "God, please get me out of here."

I found myself thinking, "Hold on, I'm a warrior. I'm a strong person who follows God. What am I doing with my life, to my kids, and to my parents?" God came through. He gave me the gift of my rock bottom. I had lost a million dollars by this point and had nothing to my name anymore. Any amount of confidence, dignity, or belief in myself was gone. My children failed. Then it happened: My son was hit on the head! I was devastated, horrified, and ashamed. Most of all, I was angry at myself.

- This wasn't just his toxicity.
- It was the dance of both our toxicities, and I was NOT a victim.

The next day, I took my kids and ran in the middle of the night. I was so confused and foggy that I got a speeding ticket on the way to my parent's house. I didn't mind though, because from that day forward, I committed to change. I would NEVER allow such self-inflicted negativity to penetrate my soul or family again.

I enlisted the help of a therapist, coach, and God and got my family back to Texas. I knew it would be hard because even in an abusive relationship, it hurts to leave. There was a period of grief, and the shame and disappointment that plagued my mind softened all too slowly. Getting over what I'd done to myself was one thing, but another thing altogether was the turmoil I'd served on a platter to my children. The notion of a "man" I'd shown my daughters wasn't good, and I'd truly let down my son.

Hi, I'm Jennifer, and I was a toxic people-pleaser for the first 37 years of my life. I ALLOWED such things IN because I was weak, insecure, didn't know who I was, and sought the approval of others before myself or God. I ignored my intuition over and over again.

Genesis 50:20. "You intended to harm me, but God intended it all for good. He brought me to this position so I could save the lives of many people."

That verse saved my life as my darkness turned to light. I dove into the waters of my journey of self-discovery, confidence, boundaries, clarity, love, purpose, boldness, accountability, and humility. It's a journey that should never end and lies outside comfort.

That scary, intentional space outside of the comfort zone is where growth and fulfillment lie.

I've learned a multitude of lessons in the last four years since that rock bottom, but 4 stick out the most.

1. **Follow your intuition.**

Bad things can happen when you don't listen to your instincts.

You may choose the path I took in that abusive relationship. You may let negative energy in your life or surround yourself with the wrong people. You may end up in a dangerous situation you can't get out of. On the other hand, look at this another way. You may miss important opportunities, experiences, and relationships when you don't listen to your intuition; you may also miss your calling.

NEVER stifle your intuition. No matter what your spiritual beliefs, it's a GIFT from something higher. It's also scientifically backed! Research in neuroscience and neuro gastroenterology (*) has shown that the GUT is like our second brain. The gut-brain axis is full of neural connections and communication. There's a REASON we feel things in our gut when there is danger, fear, excitement, etc. The two systems are reminding us to EVALUATE, sometimes quickly. Our bodies were built inchoately and beautifully.

Whether this is our conscience, *the Holy Spirit*, the universe's connection - or a combination thereof. Whether it's telling you to run, go forth, or explore further, it's usually right, and I've learned not to second guess that little but unexplainably strong feeling.

It can save us from hell and bring us to glory.

Isaiah 30:21, "Whether you turn to the right or to the left, your ears will hear a voice behind you, saying, 'This is the way; walk in it.'"

2. **Build a foundation with vision and belief.**

Vision is what I find to be the foundation that holds it ALL together. Vision, leading to purpose, creating clarity, which over time guarantees to increase fulfillment.

With the clarity provided by a defined vision, you paint a path. You can wake up every day, walk that path, and live with a sense of direction, embracing the easy decision-making and authenticity it creates. Clarity through vision automatically creates boundaries and rules. Without it, those boundaries can be impossible to keep!

The thing is, you have to do the work to create it and evolve it as needed. We often find ourselves stuck in mediocrity and complacency, especially in our Middle Ages. Are our lives ok? Yes, but we can feel lost. Isn't there more? Did we miss something? According to the Mayo Clinic (and many more resources), it's been shown that brain development doesn't even stop til 25, and possibly closer to 30. So it would make sense that when we hit our late 30s and 40s, we're like, wait, who am I?

It is important to take the steps to figure that out, rediscover yourself, and create the life you want and strive for. Evaluate your current situation in the key areas of life. Then, be greedy but realistic about creating the superhero version of YOU in the same key areas.

Think:

Business/Mission

Finances

Emotional Health

Mental Health

Physical Health and Nutrition

Relationships

Spirituality

And then go further:

Free Time/Hobbies

Political/Ethical Beliefs

Personal Development

Morning/Evening Routines

Community Impact

Legacy

Parenting

Travel

even Self-Care

Once you've defined what these look like as your best self, you can set backward tracking goals into bite-sized daily action steps.

The second part of this is **BELIEF**. You GENERATE what you BELIEVE you deserve. To a huge extent, what you achieve in your life directly reflects your actions and beliefs. Call it positive manifestation or ethical aim, and It can go either way.

Our brains err on the side of neuroticism, worry, and negative thinking. These negative thought processes can manifest in your life as poor self-care, anxiety, crappy self-talk, self-sabotage, rabbit holes of despair, and unnecessary failures. Those same negative thought processes can also be straight-up fear. However, unless you are in physical danger or there is a threat, fear is a waste of time! Fear keeps you in your comfort zone AND from relationships, opportunities, and experiences that COULD BE LIFE-CHANGING.

In contrast, good self-care, hope and ambition, upbeat self-talk/self-worth, and a real sense of responsibility and purpose — can present as confidence, success, determination, and joy.

- Do you want to channel that higher energy in yourself???
- There are practical things to do here:

Create a superhero version of yourself. An identity, An alter ego. A confident, competent, respected, credible person (+ all the other quirky adjectives you want to throw in). The AUTHORITY. Kobe Bryant did this with the "Black Mamba," as did Beyonce with "Sasha Fierce." The supercharged version of yourself comes in handy when you need to call on your higher self!

DRESS THE PART. Maintain the high standard that defines you. What does the best version of YOU wear and look like on a daily basis? Are you classy and composed, sophisticated and rugged, sexy and scientific, or sleek and solid? Or do you have a corporate job with no flexibility? DO. IT. UP. This amplifies your boldness and invitation for respect.

PROVE it with POSTURE. Stand up straight with your shoulders back. Look up. Make eye contact, be fierce, and smile with your eyes simultaneously. Make them question if you're kind, intimidating, welcoming, or a combination. This is proven to work within yourself and how you present. If you want an incredible, biological, scientific explanation for this, just read the 1st chapter of Jordan Peterson's 12 Rules for Life.

YOU DO (or, as NKOTB says, "you've got") the RIGHT STUFF. What does your highest-version superhero self do? When do you wake/sleep? What personal development habits do you maintain? What routines? What health/workout habits do you make non-negotiable? What punctuality? What spiritual habits?

AUTHENTICITY. I can't stress this enough. It's said that the biggest deathbed regret is NOT being authentic. We've all experienced this. Maybe it's conforming to peer pressure in high school, losing yourself in a relationship, and making decisions that go against your values. Or, maybe it's even broader, by following family or societal expectations that are NOT you. Stay true to your personality, ETHICS, VALUES, BELIEFS, and BOUNDARIES. Don't be that person at the end of their life that says, "I wish I would have followed my dreams, my beliefs, I wish I wouldn't have cared so much about others' opinions of me."

Let the combination of these things CHARGE your inner battery. Let it FIRE YOU UP and enable you to channel your BEST SELF. You are in control, and there are no excuses. Remember, there's no room for fear!!!! You are BOLD.

The keys here are belief and action. Even when you think you aren't ready to be this next-level version of yourself, it's imperative that you BE the person you've created, anyway. There's no room for imposter syndrome. Start living your envisioned life with the action steps, habits, and goals that align with it. You will become who you want to be. Remember, we GENERATE what we BELIEVE we deserve.

Mark 11:24 (NIV): "Therefore I tell you, whatever you ask for in prayer, believe that you have received it, and it will be yours."

3. Find your killer Ethos

Let me tell you a story about the Good Samaritan. (Gospel of Luke)

One day, a random guy asked Jesus how he could have eternal life, and Jesus told him a story:

A man was traveling from Jerusalem to Jericho. Along the way, he was unexpectedly attacked and beaten up. He had all his stuff taken and was left helpless on the side of the road. A priest and a Levite came by. These were two super religious "good guys." Surely, they'd help, right? Alas, they passed right by, avoiding the man who clearly needed a hand. Then, the "Good Samaritan" walked by, grabbed and threw him on his donkey. He took him the rest of the way into Jericho. He cleansed his wounds and even paid for his stay at the local inn.

Jesus asks: Which of these three was the "neighbor"? (And the guy asking for eternal life has his obvious answer).

That Good Samaritan had ETHOS. He showcased morality, integrity, and compassion. He was ethical, and he'd have done the same thing in another situation.

Ethos. Think ethical appeal, character, integrity and credibility, morality, and reliability. Think of it as a certain aura around you, a step deeper into your personal brand or the foundation of your business. This is your operating system. Like your vision, your Ethos provides you with direction and is another tool to keep you aligned with your path. I believe the keys to a good ethos consist of several characteristics that look a little different for everyone.

*Principles and Morals. We'll never be even close to perfect, but we can strive to the best of our ability to follow our own moral code. This makes life simpler and cleaner.

*Responsibility. Taking ownership, holding yourself accountable and reliable, and being action-oriented all play a part in responsibility. The absence of these, along with discipline and proper aim, will only leave space for someone or something else to take control.

*Credibility. The key is to live an authentic, aligned life, serving others with your specific God-given talents and tools. This requires consistency and confidence in your evolving skills and knowledge. It also requires transparent communication, integrity, staying trustworthy, and giving most people the same experience as you.

*Leadership. Providing value, being a model, and serving with knowledge and compassion.

How does one find it and forge it? As you did with your vision, take the time to reflect on and define your principles, values, and morals. Think of the traits you admire in others. Become an expert in the principles important to you. Show compassion, like the good Samaritan. Start living this way and embrace the evolution of it all. When we are true to ourselves and give value freely, we receive exponential abundance in return.

Titus 2:7-8 (NIV): "In everything set them an example by doing what is good. In your teaching show integrity, seriousness and soundness of speech that cannot be condemned, so that those who oppose you may be ashamed because they have nothing bad to say about us."

4. Seek wisdom from God to find your purpose, and follow the adventure calling you forth

Perhaps the most important lesson is what I consider the meaning of life to be: to find your God-given purpose and serve others through it. We are here to find OUR meaning and to be a beacon of light to others. Success is defined differently for everyone, but one thing about success is also true for everyone. Success alone is not enough. It needs to be accompanied by servitude, something transformative, in the form of a mission-based purpose. That combination is what truly leads you to fulfillment.

God has provided us with the opportunity to find this meaning, this purpose, and use it. In order to do this, we have to LISTEN, and follow where we're called.

Take Abraham, for example. His life didn't end with 'retirement." Life didn't really start for him until he was in his 70s, sipping tea and living the good life. That's when he heard God call him to adventure, his true purpose. He was to find a new land, Canaan (Israel). Did he question it? Yes! But through his faith, he obeyed and moved with his wife, Sarah. The journey was treacherous, through famine and conflict with other tribes. A new baby was born to Sarah's handmaid, with her blessing, as Sarah was barren.

There was times Abraham doubted, feared, lied, and made mistakes. Along the way, God made him a promise to bless him with descendants as numerous as the stars in the sky and to give them the land of Canaan as their inheritance. This seemed surreal and also impossible because of Sarah's infertility. However, God provided as He does, and Sarah (90 years old!!!!!) gave birth to Isaac (future dad to Jacob), heir to the covenant.

Then, God tested Abraham's faith by requiring him to sacrifice Isaac. He obeyed faithfully, so the angel of God came, and a ram was given in Isaac's place. Thus, the promise from God carried on even today. Abraham died at 175 years old and is revered as the patriarch of faith in Judaism, Christianity, and Islam, with descendants as numerous as the stars.

Purpose doesn't stop after high school, after kids, or even at retirement. MAYBE it is to be pursued until your last day. MAYBE pursuing it makes us live longer. It's our job to LISTEN and GO FORTH to where He's calling us.

Destiny and fulfillment are calling you. Will you listen to their voices? Run as fast as you can towards it. "RUN!!!!"

Matthew 7:7-8 (NIV): "Ask and it will be given to you; seek and you will find; knock and the door will be opened to you. For everyone who asks receives; the one who seeks finds; and to the one who knocks, the door will be opened."

***

To contact Jennifer:

LinkedIn: www.linkedin.com/in/jennifer-jehl-coaching

Instagram: https://www.instagram.com/jenn.jehl/

Email: jenniferjehl@yahoo.com

Lucie Leduc

Lucie combines her expertise as a professional leadership coach with the insight of an experienced executive. She has over twenty years of management experience in the media industry and ten years of professional coaching with executives and managers in various fields, including the last six years in the technology industry. She is well-equipped to understand the challenges related to leadership skills development and team coaching in a changing environment.

After many years of extensive management experience, during which she was recognized as an engaging and motivating leader who was dedicated to fostering the growth of her people, she chose to reinvent herself.

When the media industry was in decline, she saw the next career path that would honor her values, potential, and bilingualism at the service of the leaders. She followed her heart and gut feeling and embarked on coaching training with New Ventures West (Convivium), where she obtained her professional certification in integral development in 2014.

Committed and straightforward, Lucie is an outstanding ally in fostering human development, leadership, and sustainable change within your organization.

Leading with Curiosity:
A Story of Growth and Adaptation

By Licie Leduc

Whether you're an entrepreneur, manager, or executive or want to become one, I hope my story offers you some new perspectives to explore and will help you avoid some painful pitfalls on your leadership journey.

In 2014, newspapers and magazines were on a downward slope with the advent of Google, Facebook, and all the new digital platforms. We closed a few Canadian dailies last year, and I was asked to meet the big boss on Monday. My heart was pounding, and my palms were sweating all weekend, trying to anticipate what was coming and knowing deep in my gut that something important was about to happen. My Vice President position was abolished due to restructuring.

I had to reinvent myself. Above all, I loved helping people grow and become more motivated to develop their skills and confidence so that they could be satisfied and happier at work.

The path of coaching through a one-year certification was opening up to me, and I wanted to make a difference. The media industry no longer offered me this possibility; I had the power to embrace my destiny and change the course of my career. Changing was an unavoidable and difficult choice, but oh so satisfying. A year later, I began my own practice by leaping into the unknown, stepping on both feet in my new life mission, and welcoming the ups and downs of self-employment as an entrepreneur.

**We have never seen a strong person with an easy past

When I was young, my mother and four brothers used to tell me that I was insatiable with questions. They were exasperated by the quantity and by the tenacious energy that animated me when they didn't answer.

These were my first steps in learning to read between the lines, reach out to others, and decode what they didn't say if I was to satisfy my growing needs and thirst for learning. As the youngest in a family of five, I had to learn to navigate everyone's differences to find my place.

I quickly realized that everyone reacted to my questions differently, according to their interests. The more I asked questions in their areas of interest, the more elaborate and interesting the answers were.

Years later, life and my father's example showed me a path to sales. I had practiced in garage sales and flea markets, I had learned the rudiments, and I didn't like to sell at any price. I validated the customer's needs and interests by discussing them and asking them a few questions to fully understand what they wanted. And I'd get reprimanded by the kiosk manager.

I was hired as a receptionist for my first permanent job after graduation, but a few months later, my ego shattered. I lost the job because I was too talkative and asked too many extensive questions. I learned the importance of professional discretion. I was furious with myself, banging my head and gnashing my teeth at the thought of the next rent to pay.

Quickly applying for a new receptionist position, the boss interviewed me and said, "You've got the perfect sales profile with your assurance and presence. I'll offer you a sales position and find another receptionist. BINGO!

I began my sales career until I was assigned to manage a team because the way I asked questions and understood the customers' needs led to convincing results that were highly lucrative for the company. Not to mention my determination to feed myself and put a roof over my head, my ego was delighted with this promotion; it was the first test to overcome my beginner's candor in management.

I quickly had to manage six people who were older and more experienced than me, with no experience other than my two years in customer service and my successes under my arm as a shield, not to mention the challenge of the 90s of being a young woman among seasoned lions, enduring discrimination and judgments about my ability to lead the team with a diaper up my ass, as they used to say behind my back. Candid and unaware of the envy I aroused in some and the sense of injustice I activated in others.

I didn't help my cause; like any new manager, I tried to modulate my representatives to my own model. I wanted to create change and do things my way, to make my mark by trying to lead people and change them instead of recognizing their potential and using it as leverage.

I wanted to reproduce my winning recipe, underestimating how different others can be and resisting any form of change because, in the end, humans don't like to leave their comfort zone, which represents their personal security, but I hadn't learned that yet.

** Behind every problem, if you look carefully, often lies a refusal to change.

I dictated the way I saw things, and the title made me more decisive with the directions I gave. I hadn't considered validating what was working well and what could be improved. I didn't want to question what I knew or what they wanted to achieve.

So I hit the wall and was accused of manipulating to get my way, not respecting their wishes and ways of being, and upsetting what was already working for them. The older ones and my boss could see my confusion and my desire to hide my weaknesses, and tried to make things even more positive:

"Don't worry, it'll get better, everything will work out," making me see the positive result, which made me feel even more hurt and isolated.

With experience and several training courses, I understand what positive invalidation is and how people are well-intentioned and create more harm than good by not accepting the shadow that arises for what it is. The simple act of acknowledging that it's difficult lessens the emotional burden and offers the support needed to move forward.

I remember coming home a few times and crying with discouragement, telling myself I'd never make it. I hadn't chosen to manage people; I'd been offered it, and my ambition had seized the opportunity. I felt like a victim, and I resented being rejected and isolated from my former colleagues, whom I'd befriended as peers at the same level before and who were keeping their distance from me now.

On the road to professional advancement, I had forgotten my curiosity and ability to reach people where they were, not where I wanted them to be, for my own sake and to make sure I didn't disappoint my boss, who had trusted me.

**I hadn't yet understood that you can't want more for others than they want for themselves.

My questions and curiosity had disappeared, and I wanted so much to perform and live up to the trust placed in me that I was adding pressure, which, without realizing it, was inevitably projected onto them.

Believing I was doing the right thing, I repeated what I'd seen and experienced from the boomers: you're told what to do, because you're the boss, and you must know and definitely be right. Bam!

But at what price? I had the responsibilities, a very attractive salary for a young woman in her twenties, and the title that opened the doors to my pride and aplomb on the outside. Still, on the inside, my confidence was shaky, and my self-esteem dwindled with the setbacks I experienced and the constant self-doubt I felt. To this day, I understand that impostor syndrome is just around the corner.

**Accepting my limits with humility would have enabled me to go beyond them later, step back, and assess my options.

When I returned from maternity leave, I was told that my team had been merged with that of a male colleague because he didn't have the same family challenges as me, and it was more reliable that way. I had been reassigned to special projects without consulting me, with the privilege of having more freedom for my family!!!! A few days and nights later, I was still trying to digest what this meant.

I left the company a few weeks later. I returned to doing what I did well: customer service for two years, developing my skills nationally, refining my techniques, and resting my shaken nervous system.

I emerged from this adventure flayed and distrustful, bitter at not having been supported in my ability to develop my management skills. I felt like I'd been thrown to the wolves. Alone on my side of the arena with my sense of failure. I felt powerless in my ability to make a difference and perform through others.

**As a leader, it's not what you say that people remember but what you do.

From experience, I understand that when managers choose their path, they often have a higher level of intrinsic motivation, which reinforces their commitment and satisfaction. This motivation comes from a sense of personal control and autonomy, essential for perseverance in the face of obstacles.

On the other hand, when situations or tasks are imposed, this can lead to extrinsic motivation, where the action is motivated more by external rewards or sanctions than by personal interest or satisfaction. This can reduce personal commitment and make challenges harder to overcome, as individuals may not feel fully connected or valued in their efforts.

Having achieved a better life balance and feeling appreciated and valued for what I contributed, the ego no longer took up all the space, and my mental and physical health returned to balance.

As a colleague, people felt comfortable sharing their fears and triumphs with me because I listened to understand, not to reply or be right. People watched me ask questions with a sincere interest in learning from others, without wanting to demonstrate my knowledge at all costs or have ready-made solutions.

I had rediscovered my place in a team and the power of curiosity to move things forward, help people, and develop projects. I questioned all traditional ways of doing things with humility to understand the ins and outs that enabled us to expand possibilities and surpass our collective objectives. I experienced a lot of mutual support and inclusion in a business world I didn't know.

Two years later, I was again offered a management position in another company's division, with a younger team and a turnaround to get the ship afloat. This time I chose to accept and start differently, rediscovering my innate curiosity and open-minded questioning.

I consulted a trusted mentor to ensure a wise outside eye supported me and established what values I needed to honor in this new adventure, the lessons I'd learned the hard way, and the boundaries I needed to respect to be the leader I wanted to be.

I recognize my strengths and weaknesses and surround myself with people who compliment me. I agree to evolve collectively towards a common goal while integrating my limits and those of my people.

I took the time to explain my thoughts and needs to my new boss to see if she agreed with my way of thinking before accepting the role. She was delighted and surprised, finding this approach reassuring for a young woman in her thirties. As suggested, I took the time to find out about the team in place, their perceived strengths and weaknesses, and what was expected of me as their leader and from them before accepting the mandate. Now well aligned, as much as possible, I could move into action and hopefully not repeat past experiences.

It was a new beginning, and I was both excited and feverish because I had chosen to try another management experience and give myself a second chance. Despite all the doubts I felt, the butterflies in my stomach gave me the wings to fly off again into the unknown, with the hope of helping people and building a solid team with a little more maturity and humility.

Throughout my career, I've held nine different management positions, this time climbing the ladder gradually, finding guides who could see my potential and the gaps I needed to fill, and preventing me from falling back into my performance-at-all-costs reflexes.

When I arrived to support a new team, I took the time to establish trust as a priority and to validate the current situation and the one desired by the team, ensuring it was in line with management's expectations. Establishing psychological safety, where everyone had the right to express themselves with respect and authenticity, was a recurring factor that brought great satisfaction to all parties and a real connection with people over the course of the different mandates.

We took the time to listen to people, ask insightful questions to read between the lines and make sure we understood the issues, and then evaluate together new possibilities to experiment with. These habits earned me a good reputation and recognition as a manager people wanted to work with, and some followed me through a few mandates.

Not everything was rosy; challenges came one after the other. Because I'd been through so much in my first role, nothing seemed insurmountable when we tackled it together, discussing the pros and cons of the situation fairly.

Recognizing what's going well and what's not is essential to a manager's credibility. Learning to communicate inclusively, moving from I to WE, contributes to the troops' commitment and motivation. They feel involved and included in the resolution.

It's often easier to note what's going wrong or what needs correcting and less frequent to value what's done well on a regular basis. Appreciation really makes others feel valued and enhances their well-being.

**How people feel after talking to you is more important than the words you use.

I've had some good successes and some memorable failures, but what I remember most are the moments of pure joy when a team achieves goals after overcoming many obstacles. It's an unrivaled feeling to share that elation, and it has helped strengthen the bonds between people and the sense of belonging to the team. Celebrating victories regularly builds confidence and boosts individual and collective motivation.

There's a way of naming things with respect and authenticity. Having the courage to say the thing will bring you respect and, eventually, more credibility. When sharing your concrete observations, speak in the first person.

Without blaming people, concrete action has much more influence and encourages people to improve and feel appreciated for who they are and what they do.

Welcoming success and failure equally and tolerating the emotional pain they cause by accepting that they, too, will pass helps us develop resilience. Failure is often nothing more than a new experience, enabling us to bounce back differently.

I've been through several different management situations with my teams. What made the difference was rallying together to overcome challenges and recognize the potential and capabilities of each individual, the company, and the market.

During a major migration of our IT system, we didn't have the resources to pull it off. I didn't know anything about IT and needed a captain to bring the boat in, but we didn't have the resources to hire one.

At a team meeting, I outlined the problem and asked if anyone had skills in this area and an interest in taking on the challenge.

Catherine, a reserved new coordinator, spoke up, voice quivering, and shared that she had a master's degree in project management and might be able to lend a hand. I could never have imagined such a gift without asking the question openly.

It was an incredible springboard for her and me in my learning process to ask for help and tap into internal potential. It also sent a very positive message to the team to come out of the shadows and dare to accept new challenges.

She needed to be reassured several times during the project, which I gratefully did. We offered others what we would have liked to receive, and this was the start of a long collaboration between us.

During a qualified hiring challenge, Kathleen contacted me directly to offer her services. She had a background in telecommunications but not in the media industry.

My director at the time had never responded to her application, and she had the audacity to directly contact me, the General Manager, highlighting her skills and asking for an interview. I agreed, saying to myself that a fighter would be a great asset to our team and that I wanted to remain curious about what this person could bring to the team.

I had to fight with her manager to make her case, but I saw in this determined person an asset and was determined to give her a chance and take the risk of being wrong. This person, very different from the others, brought a new energy and arrived without a paradigm and with an open mind, eager to learn about a new industry she had chosen. It was an excellent decision that paid off on many levels.

The Director, who had refused to hire her fell under her spell within a few weeks and recognized her fear of stepping outside the established framework. She took her under her wing and gradually trained her. Her qualities, such as tenacity, adaptability, and interpersonal skills, made all the difference and enabled her to integrate smoothly into the team.

We generally look for resumes in the same field with targeted skills, and success comes more often than not from the willingness and ability to forge connections and create a climate of openness.

My manager's reflex was to hire people who looked like her and her team members based on the same known model. This limits a team's ability to surpass itself and reach new heights. Taking risks, thinking outside the box, and daring can be a winner!

People are wary of a leader who proclaims, "We've always done it this way, and it works, so why change the winning recipe?

Being a leader who accepts their vulnerability and draws on the strengths of their team to make it happen attracts more respect than someone who claims to be above it all but is brooding about stress inside. Saying out loud that everything's fine when everything's falling apart inside doesn't inspire respect and trust. People aren't fooled; they feel the things you want to hide, and these behaviors don't inspire commitment and innovation or offer a participative and collaborative management model.

**You can not bring your team further than where you are!

The influence you exert by offering yourself introspection and the right to make mistakes is desirable because, without saying anything more, you offer your team these possibilities in openness and awareness.

In 2024, the massive arrival of artificial intelligence and the problem of employee retention, particularly with the new generation, demands an ability to adapt and welcome change with openness and curiosity.

To retain our people, it's important to skillfully listen to them, understand what motivates them, and offer them challenges that match their abilities to continue developing. Trust is essential to establishing psychological security and can be reinforced by the manager's empathy, vulnerability, and authenticity.

Surveys asking why people leave jobs have shown that a large proportion are dissatisfied with their manager, lack support from management, lack appreciation, and feel useless in their role*. Investing in developing our leaders is essential to the longevity of companies, employee retention, and succession planning. If you choose to be a manager for the title, the salary, or to please because you're afraid to say no, you risk suffering and making others feel bad because it's a job that demands attention and consideration (CARE).

I got much pleasure and satisfaction from managing teams and seeing them evolve, even if it was demanding. I chose this path because it enabled me to become a better person and taught me to continually reconsider all my assumptions.

Trusting others, accepting differences, and believing in what they bring allow greater freedom of action for all parties. It certainly won't be done as you would have executed it, and perhaps you'll be surprised and learn from them like they'll learn from you. It's a win-win situation. If you're the smartest person on the team, you haven't been able to hire the right team to compliment you; your insecurity could lead you to hire weaker people than you to feel in control. This is a common trap for managers.

Make sure you spend your time with the right people because those around you greatly impact your life. We spend a third of our lives at work. Choose people who support you and encourage you and have values and goals similar to your own and complementary strengths.

There is no clear destination on the path to conscious leadership: it's a continuous process of self-discovery and the discovery of others.

Lead by example; lead with your heart.

*(source: HR Reporter Canada)

To contact Lucie:

https://lucieleduc-coaching.com/en/

Lucie Leduc
info@lucieleduc-coaching.com
LinkedIn

Jane Williams

Sometimes, the best way through a brick wall isn't straight through it; it's around or over. These words, spoken by Jane Williams' father, perfectly represent her transformation from timid to triumphant.

At a young age, Jane was known to be intellectual and creative but shy and reserved. This condition plagued her for years until she stood in front of a crowd and realized that she didn't want to be remembered for falling apart and failing but for giving an amazing performance. The time had come to find her fire and rise to the challenge. This launched a transformation that gave her the courage and confidence to speak up for herself and fueled a successful career at IBM, where she flourished in a male-dominated industry over the next two decades. Today, Jane coaches ambitious women in IT to get clarity on their careers, claim their voices, and find their fire. After successfully climbing the leadership ladder and charting her path to success, she now helps other women rise to the idea of success in their careers.

Jane is an exceptional problem solver certified in Design Thinking, with a Master's in Information Technology and a Doctorate in Leadership of Remote Teams. She actively listens and creates order out of the chaos to help her clients clarify and capture their desired career path. Her mission is to offer a bespoke experience that combines coaching and mentorship while encouraging and inspiring women across the globe.

Rethinking Entrepreneurship: Can a Corporation be the Way to Find Your Fire?

By Jane Williams

The Solitary Hero

We're all familiar with the traditional story of entrepreneurship, where heroes battle against the odds and find wealth beyond measure, bending the world to their will. That's all where we'd like to be, but it's a tale full of drama and dragons, and anyone venturing down that path must be armed with the right tools and experience. Many fall by the wayside in the quest, and it's difficult to gather those needed tools and expertise without trial and tribulation. How can you do everything simultaneously if you're just starting your career journey?

A Different Take on the Story

Is there a way to become a successful entrepreneur without all the danger? What if a gentler approach might get you where you want to be without all the uncertainty? Launching your entrepreneurial journey with the enthusiastic support of a robust corporate infrastructure might be just the help you need.

I can see you cringing right now as you read this, and I would have as well once upon a time. But think about it: a traditional entrepreneur is an individual who starts their own business based on an idea or a product they've created while assuming most of the risks and reaping most of the rewards. How about instead of starting your entrepreneurial journey alone and armed only with great ideas, high hopes, and good intentions, you're welcomed into a world where support, resources, and guidance are all around you? It's not about conformity or "selling out" but about finding a nurturing environment within the corporate realm to find your true fire and realize your boldest dreams.

I'm embarking on an individual entrepreneurial chapter, but only after learning tough lessons in two organizations: a high-tech behemoth and an institution of higher learning. Working within these incubators gave me the confidence to try new ideas and embrace new skills, all with the support of world-class mentors. I had professional support from various disciplines, learning how to make my ideas come to life in the real world. I learned how to overcome the challenge of selling new ideas to hardened executives, network effectively, and, most importantly, reinvent myself continuously and purposefully. While my story might not be typical, perhaps you can find something that resonates as you look to build your success.

"You want me to do WHAT?"

That was my mantra during the early stages of my work life. I entered the workforce of the early 80s with a political science degree and a social work background that left me with high-minded ideas and an empty wallet. Newly divorced, I needed to strike out independently, and I grudgingly accepted my father's advice that I should join corporate life. Part of that required paying my way through graduate school to get a "real" degree, and I worked many clerical jobs that left me with a bad taste for being told what to do.

After earning a double graduate degree in business and IT management, I still balked at a corporate job. I'd seen my dad and his friends work for large companies, only to get laid off or turn to stone over 30 slow years. None of that for me! I wanted a financial safety net, but I thought I knew enough to call my own shots. After bouncing around working for small businesses, I finally settled into an IT contractor role where the pay was good, the partying much better, and I had absolutely zero political stress. I thought I had the best of all worlds: a steady income doing stuff I liked, lots of free time, and a solid marketing and sales engine behind me to ensure everything stayed that way.

Then I met the guy I eventually married, who pointed out directly and firmly that I was wasting my talent and limiting my future with that attitude. He pushed me to look for a "real job," and after much soul-searching, I found a home with a huge corporation, IBM.

I can almost feel your entrepreneurial eyes rolling at my selection. IBM built a solid reputation on corporate structure, and the blue-suited, brief-case toting salesmen (and yes, they were all men) were icons of everything I despised. However, I was fortunate to join the company after it faced an existential threat and realized change was necessary. After my initial round of interviews with a panel of execs, one chased me down to my cab and offered me twice my old salary on the spot. I was stunned but eventually accepted the offer and was immediately sent to a week-long orientation, then home with a laptop and instructions on booking plane reservations. That started a whirlwind career with drama, danger, and incredible rewards. As an IT consultant, I was in charge of selling one product and one product only, and I had to do that every day to external clients and internal management. That product was me.

At the heart of it, selling confidence in themselves is what entrepreneurs do. At IBM, I had to know enough to gain the respect and trust of CXOs in major companies across the globe. More importantly, to keep doing that, I had to sell my worth to those within the company who controlled my career path, and they were often the most challenging clients.

My entrepreneurial skills at the time were minimal. I had no social polish, couldn't outmaneuver my rivals, and had no clue how to network. What I had was an enormous pile of personal capital. I was an educated woman in a male-dominated industry. I had an excellent grasp of technology, and above all, my mantra of "You want me to do WHAT?" helped me see the value of tech for businesses and how process efficiencies cut out tons of useless work for clients and myself. I helped make money for IBM and slowly gained confidence in my abilities.

Entrepreneurial Success with a Safety Net

The culmination of my career was an assignment to an Emerging Business Opportunity unit within the company, where a small, entrepreneurial group was given free rein and a blank check to test the waters for new business. I selected and trained a global group of salespeople there and helped develop innovative solutions for retailers. We were a small start-up within a large corporation, and it was a great experience. I helped create new products, launched a new process of standardizing service engagements, and traveled the world, delivering value to a wide range of clients in many industries. I also made a good amount of money and learned to invest and manage it with little risk. On the journey, I had the support of a world-class administrative, marketing, and sales organization, access to an impressive talent pool, a fantastic business proposition, and all the technical and financial support I could handle.

When I learned all I could at IBM and got tired of constant travel, I accepted a position as CIO of my alma mater, the University of Missouri—St. Louis. There, I learned how to thrive amid bureaucracy and transform IT from a utility to a strategic asset.

Coming Full Circle

I'm retired now and pursuing an entrepreneurial venture to coach women IT executives like me. I have no professional marketing department or research and development team to help me with my product. I don't have a huge pile of cash for investment, and I'm developing a whole new support network. My sales team consists of one person, me, and my product is that same person. It took a long time to prepare to make the most of working for myself, and I would never have been successful had I not gone through the crucible of a demanding corporate career. I came out of that fire fiercely determined to use the tools I've learned to deliver quality coaching to individuals looking to advance their careers, but that's not all. I developed the skill and confidence to assemble a realistic, valuable, and marketable business. All that is possible because I put in the work to learn while doing and soaked up everything I could from the professionals I relied on as an employee. I've found my fire and can also help ignite that in you!

How do you put all this together for your specific situation? How do you find the right corporation? How do you know that you'll be able to navigate that organization and ultimately find your fire? Let's take a look at some ways to make that happen.

A quick Google search will give you countless business articles defining corporate entrepreneurship. Any company that fosters innovative activities within or across established departments can provide excellent learning opportunities for a budding entrepreneur. Different models exist within organizations looking to promote innovation and branch into new ventures. The models described below give you an idea of the breadth of approaches to corporate entrepreneurship. Is one of them right for you?

Internal Corporate Ventures

1. I was fortunate enough to be part of this at IBM. Some companies create separate and autonomous units within the organization to pursue innovative ideas and opportunities. These units often operate independently, which allows them to explore new markets, technologies, or business models. This helps companies leverage internal resources, capabilities, and expertise while mitigating the risks associated with external start-ups.

Corporate Business Incubators

2. Corporate Business Incubators are similar to traditional business incubators but are created, monitored, and staffed by corporations. The parent company provides resources, mentorship, and infrastructure to help accelerate the development of innovation and new ventures, mainly focused on strategic areas that align with the company's objectives.

Strategic Entrepreneurship

3. Strategic Entrepreneurship occurs when a company takes an entrepreneurial approach and blends that with strategic management practices to pursue opportunities that address and promote competitive advantage. This model emphasizes identifying and establishing new market niches, technological advancements, or disruptive innovations, aligning entrepreneurial activities with the company's strategic goals. AI anyone?

Open Innovation

4. Open Innovation targets collaboration and partnerships with external stakeholders, including customers, suppliers, universities, and start-ups, to access and leverage external knowledge, ideas, and resources. Companies adopting this model actively seek external partners for innovation, incorporating external solutions into their products, services, or processes, and often engage in co-creation activities.

These models offer many opportunities for corporations to foster entrepreneurial activities and drive innovation within their boundaries. That's necessary for any company to survive these days, and those that combine elements of these models or adapt them to suit their specific contexts and objectives recognize the importance of entrepreneurial initiatives in maintaining competitiveness and sustained growth.

I picked a company, now what?

Do you see any of these opportunities in the company you're with now? They might be hidden or flying under the radar, so poke around, ask questions, and see if you can find a way to connect and share your ideas.

If you're already part of a company with an innovative approach or objectives for entrepreneurial units, research and find out where and how that happens. If nothing cool is happening, maybe you can start something.

Once you've done that, it's time to use all that pent-up energy. Ask yourself these questions, and really think about the answers.

- Do I have a great idea? Is there some venture or opportunity my company is missing, and does that align with the organization's strategic goals?
- Do I want to help develop a great idea? Can I partner with other intelligent people within the company to create the next great product or service?

If you answered yes to either of these questions, then continue by asking the following:

- Who's in charge of entrepreneurial ventures in my company? How do I get to know them?
- What resources are available that I'll need to pursue my objectives?
- How can I convince my leadership that I'm an excellent fit for an innovative program?

Find Your Fire and Fan the Flames!

I coach women executives in the IT industry. Some of them are dying to have their ideas heard and to be part of creating new initiatives for their company, while others love where they are and have other channels for creativity. If you're in a great organization now and want to hone your entrepreneurial skills, either for advancement or preparation for your next solo chapter, focus on these activities. You might notice that these points also pop up in purely entrepreneurial circles - there are many similarities!

1. Build Your Network: Networking is crucial in both the corporate and entrepreneurial worlds, so actively seek mentors, sponsors, and peers who can offer guidance, support, and the spark of a new idea. Look for colleagues who can provide diverse perspectives and insights.
2. Take Every Opportunity to Learn: Stay updated on industry trends, emerging technologies, and entrepreneurship and corporate innovation best practices. Learn about your leadership - what keeps them up at night? How can you help them be successful? Above all, stay focused on your organization's strategic goals and look forward to the next great idea that fits.
3. Seek Discomfort with a Growth Mindset: Develop skills beyond your core expertise, including leadership, strategic thinking, negotiation, and problem-solving. Look for opportunities to lead or participate in your organization's cross-functional projects, task forces, or innovation initiatives. Learn all you can about your company's control and power flow and how to tap into that.
4. Promote Diversity and Listen to Everyone: Sometimes, the best ideas are missed because no one tries to hear them. Advocate for diversity and inclusion within your organization. Recognize the unique perspectives and insights of individuals from diverse backgrounds, and work to create an environment where everyone feels welcome and even compelled to contribute.
5. Stay the Course: Corporate entrepreneurship can be as challenging and unpredictable as any solo venture. Stay focused in the face of setbacks and obstacles. Learn from failures, adapt quickly, and keep progressing towards your goals.

Make strategic investments in your future.

Understanding where you are now and where you want to be is so important that I can't stress it enough. It sounds trite, but one of the hazards of corporate life is "going with the flow" and letting others define your future. You must find your fire and unique voice to be a successful entrepreneur. What excites and inspires you, and how can you get others to share and invest in that excitement? Learn how to communicate effectively within your organizational culture and how to influence those who hold the keys to your future. Don't hesitate to speak up and share your ideas, perspectives, and achievements. Assertiveness and confidence are vital traits for corporate entrepreneurs, so practice effective communication and self-advocacy.

Don't hesitate to reach outside the company for help. Internal mentors and leaders are vital, but often, it's helpful to get an outside perspective on yourself, your ideas, and your approach to success. As an executive coach, I've helped many frustrated executives focus on what matters and develop the skills they already have to achieve their goals. Don't be afraid to invest time and resources into coaching or other ways to build your confidence and skill. Take a class. Join a professional organization. Talk to other entrepreneurs about their challenges and successes. Get out from behind your desk and make things happen!

Above all, Find Your Fire and ignite others with your passion and commitment!

If private coaching appeals to you, find out how to get a handle on your return on the investment. Download my free eBook "What's In It For Me? Your Guide to Coaching ROI".

***

To contact Jane:

drj@findyourfirecoach.com

LinkedIn: https://www.linkedin.com/in/janeparkerwilliams/

Michael Jacobs

Michael Jacobs has dedicated the past 24 years to empowering individuals, families, and businesses through financial education. His expertise lies in creating and implementing personalized financial strategies tailored to each client's needs and aspirations. Whether it's retiring on their terms, funding the college experience for their kids, buying a home, managing debt, supporting family members, optimizing taxes, giving back to the community, starting a business, or budgeting effectively, Mike has helped countless people navigate their financial journey.

In addition to his work with individuals and families, Mr. Jacobs also collaborates with small, medium, and large companies to develop corporate financial strategies. These strategies encompass various aspects such as startup support, growth and expansion initiatives, exit strategies, employee retention programs, and the design of corporate retirement plans and benefits packages.

With a diverse background that includes owning a mortgage branch from 2005 to 2008 and currently owning and operating a commercial lending brokerage, Mike brings a wealth of experience to his clients. His passion for financial education is evident in his belief that true empowerment comes from teaching people how to manage their finances wisely, rather than simply providing temporary solutions.

Driven by his favorite saying, "If you give a starving person a fish, you feed them for a day, teach them how to fish and you feed them for a lifetime," Michael is committed to equipping individuals and businesses with the knowledge and tools they need to reach their long-term goals and dreams.

My Journey as an Entrepreneur
Wisdom Gained from Lessons Learned

By Michael Jacobs

Initial advice from current (52-year-old) Michael Jacobs to 10-year-old Michael Jacobs just starting out on his path to entrepreneurship. As a licensed securities and insurance professional whose desire is to make a difference in overcoming a HUGE LACK OF FINANCIAL EDUCATION IN THIS COUNTRY,

1). Pay attention to the journey.

2). Always think outside the box.

3). Find a mentor.

4). Don't underestimate the power of negotiation.

5). Always be willing to serve first.

6). Never lose sight of the role your family will play in your journey.

7). Continue to learn from your fascination of the manipulation of money.

8). Last, but certainly not least, be appreciative of the legacy you will build and how you are able to use your insurance and securities licenses to empower people to assist you in the creation of their individual, family, and small, medium, and large size companies personal and corporate financial strategies.

10-Year-Old Mike

THINK OUTSIDE THE BOX

I'd like to dedicate my introduction to entrepreneurship to my parents Ivan and Rebecca Jacobs. They unknowingly taught me the first lesson in being an entrepreneur, THINK OUTSIDE THE BOX.

Every year, the elementary school I went to in North Babylon, NY took the 5th graders to Washington D.C. to go see the monuments, museums, etc.... I brought the permission slip to my parents, told them the cost of the trip was $250 and then I would hear the words which would change my life at the age of 10. "Go raise some money and we will match you dollar for dollar"

I remember thinking to myself, "I'm 10, what am I supposed to do?" My parents were like, "Don't worry, you'll figure it out" 40-some-odd years ago, apparently, it was safer for a child to walk around the neighborhood. This was right around the time when returning cans and bottles at $.05 a piece was being introduced.

My introduction to the power of numbers. I remember thinking $250 would mean 20 cans per dollar X $250 would be 5000 cans, damn! Then it occurred to me, I live within ½ mile of 3 baseball fields, it was early May, and the trip was in June. Little Leagues were going on for baseball. I noticed that each field had 3 games a day. Each team seemed to be going through about 30 cans a game, so $1.50 per team X 2 = $3.00 per game X 3 games a day X 3 fields is $27.00 a day.

Problem number 1. "How would I collect the cans?" I went up to the coaches and explained what I was doing and why I was doing it and asked, "If I bring you some trash bags, can you put the cans into the bags, and then I'll come and pick them up after the game?" They were all like "Sure, no problem"

Problem number 2. I'm 10, "How do I cash them out?" Fortunately, my sister, Ronne, who happens to be 8 years older than me, knew the owner of the Deli located at the end of the street where I grew up. Ronne went in and explained to the owner what I was doing and why I was doing it and asked if he'd be o.k. with cashing me out of the cans. He was like "Sure, no problem. Just have him bring them in"

Within 10 days, I'd raised $270 and my parents, true to their word, matched me dollar for dollar as a 10-year-old, I was walking around DC with $290 of spending money. Another valuable lesson was recognizing resources and delegating tasks I could not do myself. I was also fortunate that I had people who wanted to see me succeed.

10 Through 18-Year-Old Mike

BASEBALL CARDS AND COLLECTIBLES AS COMMODITIES AND THE IMPORTANCE OF NEGOTIATING

Over the next 8 years, I would learn the art of negotiating through a trade between my Aunt Barbara and Grandma Sally, which I would implement into the wonderful world of sports collectibles which would ultimately pay for my first car. I would also hear the words from my Uncle Glenn that would reinforce my entrepreneurial journey. Like many kids, I collected baseball cards, which to borrow a term from my current profession as an insurance and securities licensed professional, are commodities that can be traded, increase and decrease in value.

There I am sitting in my grandmother's house, my aunt had this rather large gold necklace, not like one you'd often see athletes wearing and my grandmother had this beehive-looking gold ring with diamonds, each worth several thousands of dollars at the time. I sat there and watched them negotiate for the better part of 30 minutes. They were trying to increase the perceived value of each piece, but more importantly, figure out the importance each one saw in the other.

As I mentioned earlier, many of my friends and I got into collecting sports memorabilia, mostly sports cards, a lot of baseball cards. In many ways, this was the first non-family, non-religious community I was part of. It consisted of my friends, my brother Robert, sports card shops, sports memorabilia shows, vendors, etc... This was the first network I'd built.

Looking back on it, I wish I had paid more attention to the value of setting a goal, back then my goal was to obtain the 1952 Topps Mickey Mantle Rookie card (worth roughly $60k in the mid-1980s, now worth roughly $2.5 mil in mint condition) The cards from the 1950s and before were worth more because they were rarer and harder to find in mint condition. I was spending a lot of my allowance buying newer mint condition cards which I would trade for older lesser condition cards because they were easier to trade and build value.

For 8 years, I was trading with my friends, riding my bike to the sports memorabilia shops, and my brother and I would drive to the local, state, and regional collectible shows. I was trading newer cards for older cards back up to the "hot" cards of the time back to the older cards, all with the goal of owning the 1952 Topps Mickey Mantle card.

There was a 1951 Bowman Mickey Mantle card which I had, not mint condition, but still worth about $6k at the time. Fast forward to me at 18 years old, having amassed several of the older rookie cards, newer valuable rookie cards, time to reach my goal. My brother and I went to the annual card show in Atlantic City, a place where if you were going to find something of the rarer variety, that's where you were going to find it.

I was now being presented with my first opportunity to "syndicate" a deal (pooling resources for the purpose of completing a deal). THERE IT WAS. My 1952 Topps Mickey Mantle rookie card. (granted, probably rated at an 8, not mint, but still...) I had brought all my valuable cards and a few hundred dollars. I knew I might fall short of what the vendor was looking for, so I asked my brother to pool resources with the cards and the cash he had. So, let the negotiations begin. After about an hour, we fell $200 short. I can't describe the pain I felt. 8 years of my life to fall short by $200.

Oh, the words my uncle Glenn said to me "Mike, working for other people sucks, DON'T DO IT !!" Both sets of my grandparents owned their own businesses, my Uncle Lewis owned his own business and to this day, soon to be 87 years old, incredibly sharp still finds himself negotiating deals. My dad, my Aunt Barbara, and my Uncle Glenn were in real estate in NY for the better part of 35 years, so yes, I took his words to heart.

19 Through 30-Year-Old Mike

ENJOY YOUR ENTREPRENEURSHIP

I attended and ultimately graduated from Towson State University in Northern Baltimore, MD. During my sophomore year, I answered an ad for an internship filing artwork for a company that did screen printing, embroidery, and ad specialties. After three weeks, they asked me if I wanted to go sell T-shirts at the Orioles games outside of Camden Yards, you didn't have to ask me twice.

Before I knew it, I was the T-shirt guy at Towson State, I was selling at Preakness, the Caribbean Fest in New York, I was overseeing sales teams, I was wholesaling products, creating my own products for events like when Cal Ripken broke Lou Gehrig's consecutive game streak and when the Pope came to Baltimore. I was meeting hundreds if not thousands of people. Through the advertising specialties, I was becoming the go-to guy for anything you'd want to put your logo on. I was building a network.

The two events I mentioned in the previous paragraph taught me an incredible lesson about creativity and provided me with my first real lessons about being an entrepreneur. My then-business partner and I created a shirt to commemorate the lead-up and eventual breaking of Lou Gehrig's streak. We retailed the shirt outside of Camden Yards as well as wholesaling to almost every vendor outside the stadium. We netted about $14K in two weeks. This was in September 1995.

Roughly a month later, the Pope was coming to Baltimore, I was coming off a huge win and all of the vendors wanted to know what I was creating to commemorate the Pope coming to town. My original thought was "Nothing". I thought it was in bad taste, but I did remember hearing how people were selling out of everything in Philly, New Jersey, New York, etc… I wound up caving in and designing a shirt that looked like it came from the Baltimore Sun, I did 50 dozen of them.

Lesson number 1, I should have sold these shirts to the vendors, I wound up consigning them. PROBLEM – 2.5 million people were expected to attend, but they shut down many of the roads and had only 250,000 people show up. Obviously, my shirt wasn't the only one being sold out there. There was a vendor who came from D.C. with 50,000 shirts. I could not believe what I was seeing.

Their shirt had the Pope rising up out of a sea of crabs with a can of Old Bay in one hand and his scepter in the other. I don't consider myself religious, but even I thought that, while kind of funny, was in bad taste. Nonetheless, not more than 30 minutes after the vendors realized what was happening, they wound up selling their shirts 10 for $5.00 to try and dump them. Long story short, because I consigned my shirts, I got stuck with 45 dozen of them.

Welcome to entrepreneurship. I had to get creative in how to sell them, I wound up going to some of the local churches offering to do a fundraiser where the churches would sell the shirts for $10.00, keep $5.00 and I'd get $5.00. I went from 45 dozen shirts down to 15 dozen. Now I was going from clever to a little bit desperate. I wound up having to wait almost 7 months before having another opportunity to sell the rest of the shirts. Fortunately, the Pope was only on 1 side of the T-Shirt. I wound up putting Bob Marley smoking a joint on the other side and went up to New York for the Caribbean Fest. I had forgotten 5 dozen of the 15. The 10 dozen I sold up there were gone in 45 minutes.

In a last-ditch effort, Preakness was less than 3 weeks after the Caribbean Fest, so I added "Preakness Mon" on top of Bob Marley smoking the joint with the Pope on the other side and sold the last 5 dozen shirts in under 20 minutes.

<u>30-Year-Old Through Current Mike</u>

SERVE YOUR WAY TO SUCCESS THROUGH COLLABORATION VERSUS COMPETITION (CREATE WIN – WIN SITUATIONS)

The first rule of business, if you want to have a successful business, you must serve one if not both of two purposes. Fill people's needs and/or fill people's wants. THERE IS A HUGE LACK OF FINANCIAL EDUCATION IN THIS COUNTRY!! For the past 24 years, I have been empowering individuals, families, and companies (small, medium, and large) to assist me in the creation of their personal and/or corporate financial strategies.

During these 24 years, I've seen financial products come and go, and tax laws change, but the one thing that remains consistent is the HUGE LACK OF FINANCIAL EDUCATION IN THIS COUNTRY!!

Let's face it, for the most part, schools don't teach us "How Money Works" and definitely not how to make money work harder for us than we had to work for it. If our parents aren't wealthy, more than likely they can't teach us. You're probably thinking, "There are millions of pages of information on the internet." True, but the problem with the internet is that we are at the mercy of the intent of the information versus the content.

My industry seems to have a belief, keep information as complicated as possible, if they don't understand how "Money Works" they'll keep coming back to you. I believe if I do my job properly, I will have educated my clients to the point that they can tell me what they want me to do for them and why, instead of having to rely on me telling them what to do. Part of my passion is helping people to answer the following question: "If I could help you to achieve your top five financial goals, what would they be?"

Retiring on your own terms, Funding the college experience for your kids, Proper protection to include: your Life, your Ability to replace income, your Assets, Long-term care for you and your parents, as well as Legally paying less in taxes, Starting a business, Making a major purchase, Becoming debt free, Being more Philanthropic, Traveling, etc…

A core philosophy of mine is "All money serves a purpose, not all money is created equally". For instance, if you were to look at the FAFSA form (Free Application for Federal Student Aid), you will find a section discussing "Includable Assets" and "Excludable Assets", depending on how you structure your income and savings for college, the difference can mean as much as $10's of thousands if not $100's of thousands of dollars in additional student aid.

Another example of this is when the government tells us, "When you earn income, you have two options, you can pay us now or you can pay us later, but oh yeah, you're going to pay us those taxes" However, when it comes to after-tax money (your paycheck) and depending on what you do with that money, there's a third option, TAXED ADVANTAGED (If done correctly, TAX-FREE (AGAIN, ON THE GROWTH OF THE AFTERTAX MONEY used to generate the growth) (I am not a CPA, nor do I play one on TV.) Two of the most readily available examples of this are the Roth platform for retirement accounts and certain permanent cash-value life insurance policies, both are part of the excludible bucket mentioned in the previous paragraph.

Taxes happen to be one of my least favorite words. They're also one of the biggest blind spots to our wealth. Think about it, we pay taxes when we earn (Income tax) when we spend (Sales Tax), When we invest (Capital Gains Tax), when we save (Income tax) and last but not least, potentially when we die (Wealth Transfer, Inheritance, and/or Death tax) (3 different names for the same tax)

I have found that when wealthy people want something and scream loud enough, they tend to get it. While life insurance has been around for over 150 years, how you can use it and what you can do with it, has evolved dramatically over the last 30 or 40 years. In the 1980's the wealthy decided to press for certain things: Student loans were running in the 2 percent range (they wanted to be able to structure their money to increase their ability to get student loans so they could leverage 100's of thousands of dollars of inexpensive money; similar to why you'd buy real estate)

SINCE 60 % of this country winds up in divorce another thing they wanted was a way to LEGALLY hide money from their future – EX. So, then they said, "If done properly, bankruptcy can be used as a financial instrument." "If there was a way, I could LEGALLY hide at least parts of my assets (the cash inside the life policy) from my creditors, that would be GREAT."

Then it was like "I am not a fan of this whole tax thing going on (refer back to 3 paragraphs ago for the reason) I need a workaround." "I'm willing to pay interest on a loan that I may not be required to pay back, instead of paying taxes on the gain of my withdrawals." "It would be even better if I could somehow borrow money from my policy, earn interest on the loan, and use that same money to potentially earn money elsewhere." "Almost like becoming my own bank. Oh, and if it should happen to come with a death benefit, even better."

We have the wealthy to thank for all the things which can be done with life insurance while you're alive, instead of having to wait for death.

Did I mention that the youngest client I implemented this strategy for was 1 day old at the time? My oldest client was 97, proof that it's never too early or too late to start creating strategies to have a clear vision of how to achieve your goals. When appropriate, utilizing these types of strategies along with other financial instruments can go a long way to answering the question "If I could help you to achieve your top 5 financial goals, what would they be?"

***

To contact Michael:

Cell: 443-506-3841 (Best used for texting)

Email: Michael.jacobs@tfaconnect.com

LinkedIn - https://www.linkedin.com/in/michael-jay-jacobs/

https://calendly.com/mj-financial-strategy-call/90-minute-financial-strategy-session

Onyx Jones

Mrs. Onyx Jones, who was once a homeless single mother, is now a prosperous entrepreneur, author, financial coach, and wife. She also retired from city government after twenty-six years of experience in accounting/finance. Mrs. Jones has a Bachelor's Degree in Entrepreneurship and a Master's Degree in Professional Accountancy from Wichita State University.

As a Finance Director/CFO/City Treasurer for cities in the Southern California area, Mrs. Jones handled investment portfolios of over 100 million, did financial analysis for capital improvement projects worth millions of dollars, successfully refinanced over $500M bond debt, and reduced cities' debt service payments by more than $100M (NPV). Mrs. Jones also served as a Board of Investment Trustee for the Los Angeles County Employees Retirement Association (LACERA), a $74 Billion dollar retirement agency.

Mrs. Jones has a remarkable story about how she overcame homelessness and achieved success through resilience, determination, and faith. Her story shows that success is not only about money but also about having peace and fulfillment in every area of life—family, faith, fitness, and finances. Her ideas of building a Circle of Wisdom, finding your life's purpose, and working with passion are helpful and offer encouragement and direction for others who are pursuing their own goals.

31 Days to Prosperity

By Onyx Jones

In the year 2000, I was a single mother with a three-year-old daughter, homeless due to leaving an abusive relationship. My aunt offered to lend me some money and said my daughter and I could sleep on her living room floor. Despite our circumstances, my daughter was blissfully unaware, knowing only her mother's love. I had dreams of success, but the path was unclear.

Despite hardships, I completed college in 1998, earning a master's degree in accounting. My daughter was born during my final year of college, and I had to take my finals in the teacher's lounge a week after her birth. I insisted on completing the semester, knowing my degree would benefit her. I thought success would follow graduation, but I had to learn to permit myself to succeed.

Childhood experiences have taught me to stay under the radar. In elementary school, I was bullied for my intelligence and appearance. These experiences conditioned me to expect challenges and to feel small.

Fast-forward to 1999, and I was still flying under the radar. My daughter and I were sleeping on my aunt's floor while many of my peers from my master's program were flourishing. I knew then that, somehow, I had to unlock the keys to success.

From 1999 to 2023, I found peace in my life, body, heart, children, income, and husband, Kevin. I learned that successful people think differently and focus on what works. My present-day looks much different than my life in 1999. Currently, I have retired from a prosperous twenty-five-year career in Finance; I'm blissfully married to the man of my dreams, we live in a million-dollar home, and I have the most amazing kids a mom could ask for. Through my life experiences over the twenty-four-year period, I identified thirty-one principles to create a prosperous life. I have captured those principles in my book "Thirty-one Days to Prosperity." You can pre-order a copy of this book and find more information on my website: www.onyxjonesbooks.com.

I will share three of those thirty-one principles here.

Principle One: Create a Circle of Wisdom. Surround yourself with successful people. After graduating from college, I started a small bookkeeping business, but it struggled. I was not adequately equipped, and my father encouraged me to change my environment and surround myself with successful people. This drastically shifted my vision.

Principle Two: Get Clear on Your Life's Purpose. Finding your purpose can be challenging, especially when distracted by relationships, money, or other external factors. I will share a story about how I lost focus on my purpose and eventually found it. I will also provide some advice on finding your purpose and living a fulfilling life.

Principle Three: Manifest your dreams. Manifestation is the process of bringing something into existence through your thoughts, beliefs, emotions, and actions. It is based on the idea that everything is energy and that you can attract what you want by matching your vibration with the frequency of your desired outcome. Manifestation is not magic or wishful thinking; it is a natural law of the universe that works for everyone, regardless of your background, circumstances, or level of awareness.

Let's explore each of these principles in more detail.

Principle One: Create a Circle of Wisdom

A "Circle of Wisdom" is a supportive community of friends, associates, or loved ones who are successful.

After graduating from graduate school in 1998, I took a leap of faith and started a small bookkeeping business. As a newcomer in the industry, my business income fluctuated, and I worked long hours for just enough income to get by. My living expenses increased as my daughter grew older, and our needs changed, leading to a very minimal life. Complicating matters further, I engaged in relationships that were detrimental to my growth. When my life spiraled out of control and my business suffered, my dad encouraged me to change my environment and surround myself with people who had positive attitudes, who were already prosperous, and who could offer sound advice.

So, I moved from Kansas back to California. This drastic change allowed me to shift my vision and see a different possibility for my life and financial situation. My Dad introduced me to people who had thriving businesses and owned multiple properties. I was eager to learn more. The revenue from my accounting and consulting businesses was no longer supporting me, so I was open to learning all the ways I could increase my monthly income.

As you identify people to include in your Circle of Wisdom, it's essential to be selective. You would not want someone who is critical, negative, and creates obstacles for their life or for yours in your Circle of Wisdom.

So, how do you create a circle of wisdom with the right people? Here are some tips:

Surround Yourself with Positive People: Seek out individuals who radiate positivity and possess skills you aspire to acquire. These individuals typically offer empathy, guidance, and motivation, encouraging others to pursue their dreams while actively achieving their own. They accept negative situations, learn from them, and move forward without dwelling on the negativity. Include people in your inner circle who will support you, offer constructive criticism, celebrate your successes, and help you grow professionally and personally.

Connect with a Spiritual Guide: This could be a spiritual leader, pastor, yogi, or a close friend. Finding someone who can help you become spiritually grounded can elevate your life to a new level of understanding and existence. Interacting with them should stimulate the release of endorphins and serotonin in your brain, enhancing your mood and clarity of thought. Whether you're listening to this spiritual advisor through a video or conversing with them in person, their insights should help you refocus your mind, perceive situations from a different perspective, find solutions effortlessly, and connect with your higher self.

Find a Companion to Share Laughter: Laughter is often considered the best medicine, and research supports this — laughter reduces stress hormones in the body and relaxes muscles for up to 45 minutes. It also burns calories, boosts immunity, and protects your heart. Seek out people in your life who make you laugh. This could involve chatting over the phone, watching funny movies together, visiting comedy clubs, or exchanging humorous YouTube or TikTok videos. The key is to enjoy, smile, and laugh.

Engage with Someone Who Shares Your Passions: To boost your happiness, find people who enjoy the same activities as you. Whether skiing, swimming, jet skiing, or dancing, it's time to let loose and enjoy. This could mean having a pajama dance party with your best friends, going camping with a group or organization, getting involved with your local YMCA, taking group dance lessons, or whatever excites you.

Principle Two: Clarify Your Life's Purpose

In order to experience fulfillment, happiness, contentment, inner peace, and ultimate fulfillment, it's crucial to discover your passion and life's purpose. Each of us is born with a unique life purpose. Recognizing and honoring this purpose is perhaps the most critical step toward success; however, finding your purpose can be challenging, especially when distracted by relationships, money, or other external factors. I will share a story with you about how I lost focus on my purpose and eventually found it.

As I previously indicated, I started my own business after graduating in 1998. I had a clear goal of making money and helping people, and I started by acquiring a large nonprofit client, and my business began to grow. I lived in a modest apartment with my daughter, but things changed when I entered into a relationship and married quickly. I ignored the warning signs that I was headed in the wrong direction. My partner hired their relatives to help me run my business, but I soon realized that was a mistake. My partner's relatives did not bring additional skills to the business; they were very negative and added additional expenses with no additional revenues. Eventually, I was forced to close the business, and that's when I moved to California. With the assistance of my father, I formed a Circle of Wisdom (supportive Community of Friends) and enrolled in coaching programs to help me find my purpose. I learned how to heal from my past, reconnect with my values, and discover my passion. I am now happier, more confident, and more successful than ever. I have found my purpose, and I live it every day.

Here is some advice on finding your purpose and living a fulfilling life.

Tip #1: Don't let external factors distract you from your purpose. Relationships, money, or other things can be meaningful, but they should not define you or your happiness. Your purpose comes from within, and it is what makes you unique and valuable. Use self-reflection to ask yourself, "What feeling, emotion, or characteristic do I enjoy expressing the most in the world, and how do I express those qualities?" Write down your answers. Make sure you identify times in your life when you felt powerful and strong and had the power to impact others and make a difference in their lives while also protecting yourself and your dreams.

Tip #2 Write a Life Purpose Statement: Start by describing what the world would look like if you were operating perfectly according to your purpose. Do not minimize yourself or shortchange your dreams. This is the opportunity for you to clearly state what it is you were born to do. For example, in my perfect world, millions of people have purchased and read my books, people pay to hear me speak or spend time with me, and through that connection, they become inspired to live their highest potential by doing, being, and having everything they want. Once you've written down your answer to Tip #2, gather your thoughts from the previous Tip #1 and create a life purpose statement.

My Life Purpose Statement is: "I aim to teach, write books, coach people, and develop transformational seminars and courses to inspire and empower people to live their highest vision in a context of pure love and joy."

Tip #3: Pay attention to the signs and signals that guide you to your purpose. Sometimes, life gives you clues or warnings that you are on the right or wrong path. Listen to your intuition, your feelings, and your feedback. They can help you adjust your course and align with your purpose. You can use meditation to quiet your mind and explore different ideas, discover what you love to do, and potentially make substantial income from it. We are all born with a deep and meaningful purpose waiting for us to discover. You don't need to invent your purpose; it's already there. You just have to bring it to life. Developing your talents requires effort; even the most gifted musicians, artists, and mathematicians must practice, research, and maintain their skills.

However, it should feel natural, like rowing downstream. In other words, effort is required, but it should come with ease. You're probably not living your purpose if you're constantly struggling and suffering.

Tip #4: Follow Your Inner Guidance System to explore your passions and talents. Did you know that you have your own guidance system within you that can help you get from where you are in life to where you want to go? It's called your inner GPS, which works similarly to the GPS system you use in your car or phone. Once you decide where you want to go, you need to clarify your vision and lock in that destination through goal setting, affirmations, and visualizations. The steps towards your goal will keep appearing along the way in the form of internal guidance, spontaneous ideas, and new opportunities, sometimes in ways you least expect. Even if you stumble along the way, ensure you fall forward. All these images and thoughts are sending messages to the universe. If you stay out of its way—meaning you do not interrupt the process with a stream of negative thoughts, doubts, and fears—your inner GPS will keep unfolding the next steps along your route as you continue moving toward your desires.

Tip #5: Commit to your purpose and take action. Once you find your purpose, keep your mind constantly focused on what you want or where you would like to be, but don't worry about "how" it will happen or "how" you will get there. The "how" will keep showing up at the right time without your assistance. When you present your vision to the universe, which, in my opinion, is the source of all your great visions and inspirations, you will be astounded and dazzled by what the universe can deliver. Surrendering is where the magic and miracles truly happen. Be consistent and focused, and only visualize what you want to create for your life. Ask yourself, "If my life were perfect right now, what would it look like? What kind of job or business would I have? Where would I like to be living and what lifestyle would I have?" By continually doing this visualization, your visions should start to get more defined, and you will send powerful triggers to your subconscious mind to help you get there.

Ideally, you will start seeing small manifestations of experiences that you want to have more of. One day, you may find yourself at a really cool café, sipping coffee, in a nice city, on your day off, and you realize that environment mirrors precisely what you would love to experience regularly. When that happens, you need to act on it. Your purpose is not just a concept or a dream but a reality you create and live. You need to set goals, make plans, and take steps to fulfill your purpose. You must also celebrate your progress, learn from your mistakes, and enjoy the journey.

Finding your purpose can be one of your life's most rewarding and meaningful experiences. It can help you grow, thrive, and contribute to the world.

Principle Three: Manifest your Vision

After I had moved to California, formed a "Circle of Wisdom," and became clear about my purpose, it was time to start manifesting my visions because moving to California was not without its challenges. In the year 1999, I found myself homeless for about six months. My daughter and I desperately needed a place to live, so I manifested a decent-paying job so I could get back on my feet. We were able to move into a small apartment in a pretty rough neighborhood. It was far from an ideal environment. The apartment was infested with roaches, and it was unsafe for my daughter to play outside.

One night, our building was shaken by what felt like a bomb going off. Half asleep, I initially thought America was under attack. I rushed to my daughter's room and grabbed her. It turned out that a SWAT team was in our building, having blown off our neighbor's front door. I later discovered that the neighbor was wanted for murder. This incident made me realize that I needed to be clearer about the type of place I wanted to live.

So, I started envisioning owning a house in a really nice neighborhood. My first step was renting a townhouse in a better environment than we previously lived in. Although it was an improvement, it still wasn't my final vision. It took over a year, but with determination, a few miracles, and guidance, I became a homeowner in a lovely neighborhood. I had gone from being homeless to being a homeowner.

When you combine your purpose and passion, you create a powerful force that can help you manifest your dreams. Here's how:

Step #1: Look at what you would like to manifest and visualize having those things in the present; don't focus on your current circumstances. Visualization is a powerful tool that can help you create a clear and vivid image of your desired outcome in your mind. It can also help you generate positive emotions and feelings that will attract your dream into reality. You can use affirmations, vision boards, journaling, meditation, or any other method that works for you to practice visualization regularly.

Step #2: Identify the skills you use or have used when doing things connected to your passion and purpose. These are the talents and abilities that you have naturally or have developed over time. They are also the things that can help you achieve your goals and make a difference in the world. You can use a skills assessment, a personality test, a career quiz, or any other tool to help you identify your strengths and areas of improvement.

Step #3: Invest at least fifteen minutes daily to do things you are passionate about and want to manifest. Over a year, fifteen minutes adds up to more than 91 hours. The more time you spend doing things towards your goals, the more likely your goals will manifest, and the quality of your life will improve.

Manifesting your dreams is not a matter of luck or chance. It is a matter of choice and action. By following your purpose and passion, you can create a meaningful, joyful, and abundant life. You can also inspire others and make a positive impact on the world. The only thing stopping you from manifesting your dreams is yourself.

My journey from homelessness to abundance in family, faith, fitness, and finances took years. Consistency is key. You must be 100% committed. Always keep your mind focused on what you want. The universe will astound and dazzle you with what it can deliver. If you want to read more about my journey and these 31 principles, please visit my website.

***

To contact Onyx:

www.onyxjonesbooks.com.

Nathalie Plamondon-Thomas, CSP®

Certified Speaking Professional CSP®, recipient of the Most Empowering Confidence Coach in North America Award in 2023 and 2021 Canadian Presenter of the Year, Nathalie Plamondon-Thomas is a Confidence Expert, specializing in Performance and Change. She is the author of 18 books, including 12 no.1 bestsellers. She is endorsed by Kevin Harrington from the Shark Tank, Tony Robbins, Jim Britt, and Brian Tracy. She is the Founder and CEO of the THINK Yourself® ACADEMY, offering keynotes and training, leading-edge online courses, laser-focus business strategy and one-on-one transformation coaching.

Over the past two decades, she has inspired over 100,000 audience members internationally with her high-energy and dynamic presentation style, teaching neurosciences in laymen's terms. She is known for her use of metaphors, hilarious stories, and fun interactive segments to teach how the brain works, how people use it wrong, and what to do to make it work for you.

She provides simple and concrete tools for the audience to implement the knowledge right away into their daily lives, along with a multi-touch-points-follow-up-approach to ensure a longer-term impact.

She combines over 10 years of experience in human resources, 25 years of experience in sales and over 35 years of distinguished service in the fitness industry. In 2007, she was Canada's Fitness Instructor of the Year. She is on the national board of directors of the Canadian Association of Professional Speakers CAPS and received the 2022 and 2023 President's Awards.

Finances: The No.1 Cause of Stress
Think Yourself® Wealthy

By Nathalie Plamondon-Thomas, CSP®

HOW ARE YOU DOING?

Now that the pandemic is over everything is back to "normal" right? You come home at night and your spouse asks: "How was your day?" and you answer: "My day was awesome! When I started working this morning, I quickly got into the most important task on my to-do list, which was completed by 10am. I then moved on to my next tasks, and thanks to uninterrupted focused time, I had check marks on everything by lunch hour. I had lots of time to go for a long walk after lunch, feeling completely confident, relaxed and calm. I answered all my emails in the afternoon, I'm down to a clean empty inbox. There was no change today at work, and there has not been in a long time. Nothing is urgent nor stressful. I got a huge raise today although I did not need it because I already do make plenty of money and always pay my bills on time. I came home and I had time to exercise and spend time with the kids, my teenage daughter was in a great mood as usual, so was my spouse, we always have amazing quality time together and we certainly never argue about money. I have a perfect work-life balance and, oh, while I'm at it: I found $270 cash in the parking lot by my car, just like it happens every day! A perfect "normal" day!"

Is that it? That is how your "normal" days are, correct?

Not quite. You may juggle with multiple challenges at once and everything is urgent. You may be familiar with stress and anxiety and may have experienced your confidence wavered a few times. You spend your days running around like a crazy chicken and when you get home at night, you are exhausted, you have not used your gym membership in months because after taking care of your kids, homework and family stuff, Netflix with a bottle of wine sounds a lot more appealing than running on a treadmill in spandex.

Maybe you're usually a really positive person, but you may find yourself off your game.

As fast as things are going now, they will never be that slow again.

Change is NOT going anywhere.

The changes we've witnessed in the world are here to stay, and they're going to keep coming. Our "new normal" is that there *is* no normal anymore.

So, how are *you* feeling? Super confident?

WHY IS CONFIDENCE SO IMPORTANT?

What does confidence have to do with cracking the rich code? 73% of people identify FINANCES as the number one cause of stress. When we are stressed, we are not at our best. Confidence allows you to have access to your best self and be resourceful when facing the new 'normal' that we live in. When you are at your best, is when you can enjoy wealth.

True wealth is achieved when people are at their best; they can focus, find clarity, take calculated risks, control their emotions, and find alignment within themselves.

LIMITING BELIEFS

We were *all* raised with limiting beliefs, many of us around money, leading us to make the wrong financial or professional decisions. Maybe your parents told you things like: "You need to work hard for your money," or, "Money doesn't grow on trees."

These limiting beliefs can keep you from finding full financial confidence.

I'VE BEEN THERE.

When I was in my twenties, I sold a business, and I made the kind of money that could have allowed me to take it easy for the rest of my life and not have to work that hard. What do you think happened? That's right, two years later it was gone. I thought I was good with money! I was actually good at making money, but it turns out that I was even better at spending it! You see, I had this limiting belief, that *when you make more money, you spend more money.*

When I discovered this limiting belief and dealt with it head on, that was when I really started to be great at managing my money. That belief had been eating away at my confidence for years because I could never save as much as I wanted, no matter how much money I was making.

I realized that I was only responding to what I believed was true in my head.

IT STARTS WITH THE WAY YOU TALK TO YOURSELF

Everything starts with the story you tell yourself in your head. Let's go back to the days when I was just starting out teaching fitness, at a gym in Toronto. I was not super confident; I'm sure you've been there before, maybe not in a gym but in some other setting where you were brand new and a little out of your element. You're not sure what you're doing, you're not popular, you don't know anybody, or you're new in the area and haven't really found your feet yet. So, what happened between me begging my boss not to remove my class from the schedule because of the low numbers, and being awarded fitness instructor of the year for the whole country, less than a year later?

The gym was introducing a new dance program. We put together a group to demonstrate it at the next instructor's meeting of the Greater Toronto Area. So, picture this: You are on stage in front of 100+ fitness pro, all much better than you, you are really intimidated but you are "giving your all". You are starting to feel pretty good, and you can just feel all the eyes in the crowd turning towards you. You know you are drawing attention, and everyone has this shocked look on their faces! You are thinking "Oh yes, they're so impressed with my dance skills! They had *no idea* I was this good at dancing!" You're having the best time on stage and can really feel all the energy coming from the audience.

I don't know what this would do for you, but for me, it made a huge impact on my life. It was a real turning point. We finished the number, and I was *amped*. My confidence was through the roof! That performance totally changed me. I started strutting around in the gym and putting my hand up to become team leader, I was so confident that my teaching style exploded, and my classes started to get packed. Everybody was so impressed with how well I was doing.

Much later, I was chatting with one of my colleagues in the locker room, and she said to me: "I'm so impressed with you, Nathalie.

Even after what happened to you that day, you're still so confident, and you've been acting like you own the place instead of being embarrassed. Everybody really respects you because you didn't let it bother you at all."

Um, record scratch! *Excuse me?!* What was she talking about? Well, it turned out that, unbeknownst to me, I'd had a wardrobe malfunction that day, and my breast was sticking out during the whole performance. *That's* why people were looking at me with shocked looks on their faces. But for a very different reason than I thought!

But I had no idea, and for weeks afterward, I was this super confident person. Once I heard about this, of course, I kind of wanted to disappear, but only for a few minutes; by then, it was too late, I was already the queen of the gym.

One of the most embarrassing moments of my life had a much different impact for me than it might have, because I was responding to a different story in my head.

What mattered most was my *mindset around it.*

So, I spent the next decades studying the brain and neurosciences and I created a system to transform the story in our head and a process to apply it to your daily life. That is the system I shared in my 12 International #1 bestsellers, the system I work with my one-on-one coaching clients, the system at the base of my 20+ online courses and the system I share on stages around the world.

MOST OF YOUR THOUGHTS ARE NEGATIVE

It turns out that research reveal that 70% of our thoughts are negative. We spend *so much* of our time in negative thought patterns.

Imagine if we talked to people like this: "Hey, you look terrible in those jeans!" or "Wow, you must feel like such an idiot for saying that! What's wrong with you?"

No right? You would never say those things with your outside voice! We don't talk to other people like that. But that is how we address ourselves!

Who would want to be your friend if you talked to them the same way you talk to yourself?

Paying attention to your thoughts is the first step – becoming more aware your negative talk is a great start for gaining confidence.

HOW THE BRAIN WORKS

Let's talk about the two parts of the brain. First, there's the logical mind. It can process an average of five to nine pieces of information at a time. That's why you can do your grocery shopping while you're in a meeting on your headphones; you can grab a can of soup on special with one hand, keep your kid from falling off the cart with the other, and still notice the old guy in the corner that's checking out the girl in blue in the seafood department. We multitask all the time.

But imagine you're driving to a new address. The windows are down, music is on and as you get closer to your destination, you slow down to start looking for the numbers on the buildings . . . have you ever caught yourself reaching for the volume to quickly turn it down so you can 'see' the numbers better! What's that all about?

You were driving along, taking in all sorts of information without a problem: kids on the street, oncoming cars, the music, the GPS directions. But once it was time to find that number, your brain stalled. It had reached that ninth item! So down went the volume, the one thing you could control in the moment.

LIVING AT A LOGICAL LEVEL

When you live at this logical level, you're always trying to catch up. You must work really hard just to get what feels like "normal" done.

You're plugging away at work, heading towards a goal. You're aiming for a sales target, or a new contract or a promotion. You start early and you work really late. You're ambitious, and you want to upgrade your skills or take that online course. But you're busy dealing with day-to-day issues at the office, like a dispute with your staff, accounting problems, customer complaints, and IT disasters. Or you are spending countless hours trying to build a successful business as an entrepreneur.

Your work-life balance has gone out the window, and so have your ambitions; it feels like you're getting farther and farther away from the dream life you'd envisioned. It's like you want to go to New York City, but you're in an aircraft that's flying to Los Angeles. You can work as hard as you possibly can, but you will never get there if you stay in that aircraft! The key is to talk to the pilot and get them to turn around.

YOUR PERSONAL ASSISTANT

So, how do you talk to the pilot? I call it your "personal assistant".

Your personal assistant is like the pilot flying the plane. She represents another part of the brain: your UNCONSCIOUS MIND. It is so powerful. It can handle over 2.3 million pieces of information, every *second*. Your logical mind could handle five to nine only. The unconscious mind is where the power is!!

Your personal assistant is inside your head *all* the time, taking notes and making sure everything you say or think gets done. But the problem is: People get up in the morning, they look at themselves in the mirror and they say: "Oh my! I am so tired. I'm so stressed. I think I am gaining weight!"

When you think these things, your personal assistant writes it down. *Tired – stressed – gaining weight.* Got it! Then, she'll spring into action.

"Okay, **tired**: I will keep her awake all night, so she's going to be very tired in the morning. *Check!*

Stressed out: I'll make her delete a very important meeting from her calendar, that will be very stressful. *Check!*

Gaining weight: Oh, that's an easy one. I can certainly find a chocolate bar, or something deep fried for her to eat today. *Check!*"

So, your personal assistant is your pilot, listening and steering you in the direction you tell her to go. You must be really careful about what you tell them. Say what you *want*, not what you *don't want*. You're not going to call a contractor and tell her to paint your kitchen NOT blue, right? Or buy a plane ticket to NOT Mexico? That wouldn't work. Your personal assistant operates the same way.

My one-on-one coaching clients do this all the time. They keep telling me what they DON'T want. I don't want to be stressed anymore, I don't want to rush everywhere, I don't want to be impatient with my kids and I don't want to be broke. Their brain hears stress, rush, impatient and broke. Sound familiar?

I NEED TO FIRE MY ASSISTANT

I was teaching the THINK Yourself® WEALTHY program at the Shangri-La hotel and a participant came to me afterward: "Wow! I need to fire my personal assistant!" I asked her why? She said: "I am here, really determined to be better with my finances but I am always stressed about money, I am a shopaholic and when I make more money, I spend more money, so I always live paycheck to paycheck." I responded: "Let me ask if I understand you clearly. You just said that you want to be stressed about money, you want to be a shopaholic, you want to spend more when you make more, and you want to live paycheck to paycheck. And you believe that your personal assistant is not doing a great job and you want to fire her? Then she said with a huge exclamation: "Oh, it's ME that is not giving her the right orders!" Bingo.

With these limiting beliefs, let's say your savings account is starting to grow, and you're finally feeling some financial ease. But then, your personal assistant panics because you've told her you're supposed to be stressed about money! So, she says: "Uh oh, she's getting ahead and feeling comfortable, but she's supposed to be stressing about money. What can I do? I know, I'll make sure she totally fails the interview for that promotion she wants, because if she gets it, it will come with a raise, and she said she wanted to be living paycheck to paycheck. So, I'll make sure she doesn't get it. Phew! I did my job! *Check!*"

The bottom line is that words *do* matter more than you think. You need to pick them very carefully if you want to reprogram your own brain for financial confidence.

I use specific processes to do this at an unconscious level with my clients. While I cannot teach you how to do these processes by yourself, I can give you a simple two-step technique to start the process of breaking through these limiting beliefs and boosting your confidence. This is only one of the multiple tools available in the full online course THINK Yourself® WEALTHY, created in collaboration with Certified Financial Planner Lynn Williams.

THE TWO-STEP TECHNIQUE

You may have tried positive affirmations before. I'm sorry to tell you, but affirmations don't work . . . *if* you don't believe them. When you create affirmations, they must be genuine. Usually, there is too big of a gap between the affirmation and the reality. When I work one-on-one with senior executives who have a gazillion things to stress about, it won't work to tell them: "Okay, stand tall and repeat after me: 'I am calm!'" Or when I work with my THINK Yourself® WEALTHY clients in deep financial struggle, I can't make them stand in front of the mirror and say: "I am rich!" It won't work. Their personal assistant will hear the words and roll their eyes and say: "Yeah right! She's not talking to me; she must be watching a vampire movie or something because this makes no sense. I am not writing this down."

You need to go a couple steps further than just the affirmation. Here they are.

STEP 1: You need to start by reframing the negative thoughts in the past. For example, the old standby: "I am so stressed out!" Take that statement and place it in the past. Say: "I *used to* think I was stressed out all the time." Your personal assistant will hear it, and think, "Oh yeah, that's on my list right here: *stressed out*." And then she will inquire: "But wait, why are we talking about it in the past? Are we done with that? Do I scratch it off the list, or what?" Now your personal assistant is primed for a new direction.

STEP 2: Immediately follow step one with a *progressive statement*. A progressive statement starts with *I am willing to learn…* or *I am in the process of…* "I am willing to learn how to stay calm." Or "I am in the process of building a balanced life."

Another example: You want to apply for a promotion, but you doubt you will be considered. Or you have been promoted, but you feel like a fraud. You hear yourself say: "I'm not good enough to be a manager." Catch yourself! What do you say instead?

Step 1: "*I used to* think I was not good enough to be a manager."
Step 2: "Now, I am *willing to trust* myself, and figure out what I need to learn." Or "I am *in the process of* changing that."

I hope this simple tool can be one piece in helping you crack the rich code. You only have one life, invest time in yourself to be your best and unlock your full potential!

***

To Contact Nathalie :

https://thinkyourself.com/

Download the 10 Common Behaviours of Financially Confident People: https://thinkyourself.com/10commonbehaviours/

Checkout the THINK Yourself® WEALTHY online course:

https://thinkyourself.com/product-page-think-yourself-wealthy/

Download the 15 keys to Find Self-Confidence: https://thinkyourself.com/confidenceguide/

Book a free 15-minute Virtual Coffee with Nathalie

www.thinkyourself.com/schedule

Connect on Social Media

Facebook: https://www.facebook.com/nathalie.plamondonthomas

Facebook: https://www.facebook.com/ThinkYourselfAcademy

LinkedIn: https://www.linkedin.com/in/nathaliept/

Instagram: @nathaliepthinkyourself - https://www.instagram.com/nathaliepthinkyourself/

YouTube: https://www.youtube.com/c/NathaliePlamondonThomas

Clubhouse: @Nathaliept – Twitter: https://twitter.com/thinkyourselfAc

Mike Oglesbee

Mike Oglesbee is an acclaimed author and Mindset Coach helping people overcome their fears and mental health struggles since 2011, when he founded Maximized Mind, LLC. in Myrtle Beach, SC. Drawing from his diverse and unique background, Mike has created a powerful, dynamic approach to address the root causes of personal and professional struggles. Mike believes that knowledge is power and that we can empower ourselves to make positive life changes by understanding ourselves better. As a coach, mentor, and advisor, Mike devotes much of his time to helping people step into their power and reach their full potential.

From Surrender to Success: Harnessing My Hidden Potential

By Mike Oglesbee

THE BEGINNING OF A NEW CHAPTER

In the spring of 2011, I began my journey into self-development. It all started with The Secret, a book that has inspired and changed the lives of many throughout the world. This led me into meditation, self-development courses and programs, and deeper fields of psychology such as Neuro-linguistic Programming and Hypnotherapy. At the time, I was a singer traveling around North and South Carolina, making a pretty good living. However, once I discovered my talent for helping others, that quickly became a distant memory.

A friend of mine was a local chiropractor with a successful business who was open to my new interests in helping people develop and improve their minds. After seeing my success with a few of his clients, he invited me to open a full-time practice inside his facility. It was as if the red carpet was rolled out almost by magic. I felt more purpose than I had ever experienced and was excited about my new adventure.

I knew life was calling me towards some greater purpose than entertaining people on a Friday night with good music, so I stepped through this open door with the excitement of a child. And to top it all off, I married my beautiful bride just a week and a half before accepting my first client. I was on cloud nine.

Success seemed to be just a natural product of this new venture. I was stocked with clients and a support system that I was sure would propel me into the greatness I always knew was buried deep within me. Everything was happening so fast that I couldn't see or imagine my upcoming downfall. My disillusionment became apparent after six months, and my glass empire shattered.

THE DOWNFALL

I remember looking at my beautiful grey-marbled Epiphone electric guitar and Mustang amp for the last time as I handed it over to the pawn shop employee. It was the last of my prized possessions sold to raise enough money to cover the moving expenses from Myrtle Beach to my hometown three hours away, where I was forced to move my new bride and me into my parents' home. I felt humiliated and defeated.

My path to greatness quickly transformed into utter despair and failure. I hit rock bottom. It was the story of my life, after all. I always had that steady voice within, reaffirming that I wasn't deserving or worthy enough to have what I wanted. Why should I think this would be any different?

After a few weeks of soul-searching, introspecting, and trying to figure out my next move, I decided to continue trying to build my business. This time, I started with the basics: learning how to run a business. Although I knew how to perform my craft and help people, I didn't know the first thing about running a business.

As simple as this sounds, it never occurred to me to learn how to be a business owner. I was under the illusion that just being good at my technical skill of helping others was enough to succeed. This sent me on a journey of business development skills and training.

For the following two years, I spent one night away from my family working at the beach with the small amount of clientele I could gain from a state away. At the time, I was still pretty broke, so I settled for sleeping in my truck in semi-lit parking lots such as McDonalds and Wal-Mart to avoid getting robbed or harassed. Sometimes, I could afford a cheap room at a local hotel during the winter months when they were on special for $30, or my aunt would allow me to stay in her rental house along the beach.

When I wasn't at the beach, I worked in a local office trying to build some business and experience in my hometown. I was successful with many clients I worked with but faced much backlash and resistance from the community. My hometown was a small area that had not yet expanded to more modern and contemporary modalities in health and wellness, such as hypnosis, energy work, and NLP.

Before long, I received word that preachers were speaking against my work, discouraging their congregations from exposing themselves to this form of mind control. I even remember going to volunteer my time at the local soup kitchen to connect with other locals as a new business owner in town, just to get laughed at and turned away.

I knew I stood the possibility of receiving some pushback from the community and that much of it was from their fears and lack of true understanding of my work. If receiving rejection from the community wasn't enough, I also received it from my family. I was shunned, condemned, criticized, laughed at, and accused of being a charlatan. As someone who felt the sting of rejection and judgment my whole life, my initial reaction was to fight back. To declare that my work was for the good of others and that I was not practicing pseudo-psychology.

I learned that fighting back didn't help but only kept me in the line of fire. I had always heard that success is the best response to those who condemn you, so I turned a blind eye and started minding my business. It wasn't easy, but I was determined to be successful no matter the cost. I worked seven days a week creating new ideas, studying, learning, and doing everything I could to make my business successful.

In 2014, I found an office at the beach and decided to take a leap of faith. For the next two years, I traveled to work with clientele for three days each week. Now that I had my own space and was no longer renting a room by the hour, I upgraded to sleeping on an air mattress on my office floor. I purchased a membership at the local gym, where I took my daily showers. My office had a waiting room with a bathroom so I could brush my teeth and get ready before clients began arriving. Still, I felt like I was living a double life. I was helping people become happy and successful, but I was sleeping on a blow-up mattress on my office floor two nights per week.

My business was growing enough to justify being away from my family for three days per week, but my path was more painful and challenging than ever. While taking care of our kids alone and the added pressure of holding down a full-time job, our relationship endured significant strain.

At the time, I didn't understand the value of having a harmonious relationship outside of feeling a deep connection with someone. I was never good at being vulnerable and putting in the effort required to maintain a strong and thriving relationship. As someone who didn't value themselves much, I limited the stock I put into my relationship.

To make matters worse, even when I was home, I locked myself in my office away from my family, plotting ways to grow my business. I thought I had to work every hour of every day to be successful, a habit I learned by watching my father work seven days per week for nearly all my life. I was more anxious than ever, constantly depressed, and destructive towards myself and my family with my bad habits. I was running in circles without any direction. Still, I was giving others direction and helping them beat their demons with great success.

I was too embarrassed to tell anyone about my situation because I thought they might look at me differently. Like I was some fraud who was out here acting like I knew something about happiness and success when I couldn't even get my own shit together. Yet another story to reinforce that I wasn't good enough. Can you see the running theme?

Many nights, I stared out of my office window, utterly alone, asking myself, "Mike, can you do this?" I thought about the strain and difficulty I placed on my family's shoulders with my absence and thought about walking away many times. But again, something inside me wouldn't let me let go. I was so compelled to continue pursuing my business that quitting wasn't an option, regardless of how I felt.

In 2016, I was finally able to move my family back down to the beach so we could be together every day. Business was doing well enough to make ends meet, and my influence expanded. I had a steady stream of clients and was becoming a respected and well-established business in the community.

IT'S ALWAYS DARKEST BEFORE THE DAWN

While much of my work produced results, life was about to teach me one of the greatest lessons I would ever learn: the true cost of success. My delusions of success came to light in 2017 when my world as I knew it fell apart. In February, my father was diagnosed with cancer, which was the biggest thing to happen in my family. I had always feared death, but the death of my loved ones most.

From March to June, I traveled every three weeks to sit with him during his chemotherapy treatments. The best part about this was building a relationship with him for the first time. I was determined to get to know the man my father was and soak in as much wisdom from him as I could in case he didn't survive. Fortunately, he went into remission after his treatments and is doing well.

Meanwhile, in May, my wife's grandmother suddenly passed away one morning after breakfast. This came as a shock to the family as she was the matriarch. The impact this had on me was significant, as I loved her dearly. After the funeral, while the family gathered at the local church to commune over a feast they prepared, I received word that my aunt, who was in surgery, was found to have stage four cancer. The doctors said they could do nothing beyond some treatments, and the future looked grim and uncertain.

If this weren't enough, I was broke once again with all the time I had taken away from work to be there for my father, the cost of traveling, and extra expenses. Under the weight of stress, pain, suffering, and fear, I crumbled. I just fell apart in the parking lot of the local park, where my wife and I decided to pull over and take a breath from all the chaos around us.

In my silent suffering, I cried to God, "I'm done! I'm done! I just can't do this anymore! I can't take it! You can leave me here at the bottom of this pit, you can take me to the top of the mountain where I want to be and have been trying to reach for so long, or you can take me out of this life completely!" I was done, and I meant it. My pain had become greater than my passion, and I just let go.

At that moment, I stopped focusing on what I wanted and what I was working for. I stopped trying to make things happen the way I thought they should. I stopped caring about the results and what was happening around me. I didn't stop caring about life and those I loved; I just let go of the expectations and results I had been working to create over the years. I decided just to accept whatever comes from whatever I do. I could no longer fight this never-ending battle of suffering and failure. Thus began my path of surrender.

Accepting that my efforts to control and change my world were futile and a one-way ticket to pain and suffering, I focused inward. I attempted to change the only thing I could control: myself. I accepted that my strategy didn't work and that continuing to use it would be foolish. With this awareness, I was finally willing to change.

I was compelled to begin a gratefulness practice by sitting in a state of gratefulness each morning for up to twenty minutes. I gave thanks for anything and everything I could think of, including my socks, shoes, toilet, lights, water, phone, and not stumping my toe as I walked past the bedpost. I didn't see any dramatic changes in my life at first. Still, I did feel lighter from no longer carrying the burden of constant worry about what was and was not happening around me.

I began to ask myself deeper-level questions, such as, "Who am I?" Who do I want to be in this world? Why do I want to be these things? What purpose do I really want to serve? What legacy do I want to leave for my children and those who follow? I was no longer trying to decide what I wanted from life or what life could give me. Instead, I began exploring what I wanted from myself and what I could give life.

I had done surface-level growth before, but it was typically driven by an external desire to achieve or attain something I wanted, like money, attention, acceptance, or respect. But none of it really worked. I had achieved many things, but nothing filled the deep void within me. Without a desire to step back into that cycle of dead ends, I was now compelled to dive deep into my soul. It was time to see what I was really made of and what potential lies beneath the surface.

Though my focus had shifted, and I was on a new journey propelled by a more profound desire for inner peace and true fulfillment, some of my most challenging times were still ahead. While visiting for my father's final treatment, I awakened to one of the most stunning and life-changing epiphanies that shook me to my core and ultimately led to my estrangement from my biological family.

Despite the pain and difficulty of such a significant change in my life, I continued on my path of growth and self-discovery. I stayed true to my path of surrender and allowed life to bring whatever it wanted while I remained focused on using every experience as a steppingstone to a better version of myself. I adopted the philosophy that everything in life contained a gift and that it was my job to find it.

I learned to accept myself, love myself, and increase my self-worth. I began to pay attention and take care of my emotional needs rather than depend on others to do it for me, which never worked out, nor should it have. I turned my inner critic into an unshakable inner coach and began to support myself in all the ways I needed. As I developed and focused on expressing myself as the man I truly wanted to be in this world, regardless of my experiences, I noticed a shift in my external environment. I finally began to forgive myself and others, and my life became like a magic show unfolding in directions I never knew existed. For the first time, I was finally being the man I always knew was within me, and that's when my world changed.

A NEW WORLD

Much to my surprise, it was only when I had lost everything, including myself, and let go of trying to make everything happen that I began receiving everything I had always wanted. My business exploded into six figures, my marriage began to thrive, and I was finally happy and enjoying my life. I could say I was doing well for the first time. I was no longer depressed, anxious, or constantly struggling.

My dreams were finally coming true, and I could hardly believe it. At first, I was waiting for the other shoe to fall, but it never did. Everything just kept getting better and better. No matter how good it got, it continued to get better. It was like I was living in some fantasy world. It's not to say that struggles were no longer part of life; they just no longer consumed or controlled me, and I could move through them with greater ease.

My experience taught me that we don't get what we want in life; we get what we are. Before I began incorporating personal growth into my life, regardless of what or how much I did to become successful, I continued to create the same results repeatedly. Sometimes, they looked different, but the same experiences resurfaced, and I was left fighting the same battles. When I finally let go of trying to force things into existence and began to work on myself, shifting my mentality of lack into one of gratefulness and becoming the man who produced the life and results I desired, I gained the capacity to create and handle what I wanted.

The greatest lesson I learned along my journey, which remains true to this day, is that growing a business or creating greater levels of success in life requires far more than taking action in the world around us. It requires, no, it demands, a greater version of us. Life is our mirror. Its reflection is unbiased and shows the true identity of every person. The only way to change the reflection is to change what is being reflected: you.

***

To contact Mike:

843-213-2597

www.MikeOglesbee.com

www.facebook.com/authormikeoglesbee

www.youtube.com/@mike_oglesbee

www.linkedin.com/in/mikeoglesbee

Luz Maria Villanueva, MA., Ph.D.,

Luz Maria Villanueva, MA., Ph.D., is a dedicated psychologist, writer, public speaker, teacher, entrepreneur, and coach. A proud mother of three and grandmother, she passionately engages with her community. Her life's mission is to explore the depths of self-identity and human connection.

Dr. Luz is the President and CEO of Discover Passion with Dr. Luz and the President and co-founder of Latinas With Purpose, a non-profit organisation. With a Master's Degree in Psychology and a Doctorate in Clinical Psychology, she has extensive experience in understanding the complexities of relationships and love.

Throughout her career, Dr. Luz has provided mental health assistance and coaching to individuals, couples, and families across the United States and Mexico. She has led numerous workshops on topics such as sexuality, self-esteem, love, and parenting. Her teaching career spans nearly a decade at Grossmont College and Southwestern College.

Dr. Luz has contributed to various publications, including a column for La Prensa Newspaper and currently writes for Latinas Con Poder magazine. She is co-authoring the book "Let's talk Sex and Money- Conversations to Reinvent your Relationships" and collaborating with 45 Latinas on a book about art and short stories. Additionally, she hosted the radio show "En Familia con la Doctora Luz," catering to the US-Mexico border audience.

Through Discover Passion with Luz, Dr. Luz offers sex and intimacy coaching and personal life coaching services both nationally and internationally via Zoom.

Passion and Grit:
An Entrepreneur's Journey through Light and Darkness.
How I Reinvented Myself, Rediscovered My Passion, and Transformed from Employee to Entrepreneur

By Luz Maria Villanueva. Ph.D.

The Tree of Life: Finding Strength in Darkness

In its pursuit of sunlight, a tree navigates two opposing forces: gravitropism, pulling its roots downward, and phototropism, urging its branches upward. Initially, the tree's journey begins beneath the surface, where its seed takes root, holding the potential for future fruits and shade. As roots extend unseen, they face challenges—darkness, rocks, aridity—expanding beyond the tree's canopy.

This hidden struggle often goes unnoticed, as observers only see the tree's upward growth. They see its fruits or shade and assume the process is effortless, failing to grasp that reaching the light requires enduring darkness, confronting resistance, and transforming beliefs. In darkness, character is tested, and personal growth occurs.

During this growth phase, some may withdraw or judge, not recognizing the importance of nurturing roots. Yet, as the tree bears fruit, these individuals may return, inspired by the tangible results. The tree's downward journey through darkness is essential for upward progress. Without embracing depths, one cannot ascend toward the light. Only the seed knows its potential for fruit or shade. You know your dream and must discover and create it.

Life is like a tree. The seed, planted in darkness, finds stability by anchoring roots while branches reach for light. People see achievements, but the struggle behind them often goes unnoticed. In darkness, struggles and beliefs transform. People may judge you during this time, but when they see the fruit or shade, they reflect on possibilities. You can't rise if you're unwilling to go down.

Just as a tree's fruit or shade, take years to emerge, so do our life's purpose and potential require time and nurturing to blossom. The seed represents our inherent purpose, growing through experiences before bearing fruit, our unique contribution to the world. Like a tree's fruit, our purpose and abilities are meant to be shared to create a better world.

For me, the topic of sex and intimacy emerged naturally. I was asked to educate in this area by jobs, friends, family, and community, which I was comfortable with. This chapter of my life is the fruit of years of work, sacrifice, and love. Even those who feel they lack abilities or have disabilities have a purpose. Nature teaches us that even seemingly insignificant elements—a weed, a larva—play a role in life's intricate web. Similarly, every person, regardless of perceived limitations, has a unique and valuable place in our world.

Embracing Passion: My Personnel Story & Transformation

Well, let me tell you, my story. I am a clinical psychologist who no longer wants to work in the clinical setting, teaching, or research.

I aspired to assist as many individuals as I could. After enduring ten years of legal struggles and grappling with clinical depression, and with no financial resources at hand, my children had all flown the nest; I found myself sharing this for the first time.

I lost my home and was left with only a salvaged car. Gratefully, my mother offered me shelter in a small one-bedroom apartment she owned.

I took two years to heal my depression without the use of medication, just using the tools I had learned from psychology, mindfulness, exercise, Landmark personal and professional development programs, Tony Robbins programs, and listening every day to motivational speakers like Les Brown, Brene Brown, Wayne Dyer and falling in love again with great sex. What! Yes, great sex and love heals.

After contemplating for a few years, I decided to pursue a career as a Sex and Intimacy Coach. It resonated deeply to my core. I wondered how to build a business without any initial funds from this passion. How could I reach and influence a larger audience than returning to a clinical setting or establishing a private practice?

What will others think? A Latina educating and coaching about sex? Doubts and potential obstacles began to surface with every step I took.

Being a woman and Latina I have faced many barriers from family, friends, including the universities that I attended.

I realized that in traditional employment, success often depends on showing up qualified and performing duties competently, with advancement for exceptional performance. My strength lay in innovation, identifying problems or untapped resources and implementing solutions. During my short tenure at a Mental Health hospital, I worked across various departments, including emergency and adolescent floors. In the emergency unit, I engaged with patients, listening to conversations and making a noticeable impact. On the adolescent floor, I introduced long-overlooked activities like volleyball and other games, sparking enthusiasm among most adolescents on the days I was there.

I served a Latino community with Spanish speakers and was tasked with leading a sex education course. The room had about 30 attendees, but ten minutes in, all the men left. Undeterred, I focused on the women. I started an exercise program and trained three women. Remarkably, the program endured for five years after my departure.

In the clinic, I designed a program for mothers who had children with challenges. As a mother to a legally deaf-blind son, I empathize deeply with them.

As a college instructor, I encouraged students to collaborate on team projects, leveraging each member's unique talents.

I experienced numerous triumphs, including writing psychology columns for a newspaper and hosting a radio show with listeners spanning the US and Mexico.

As a mother, I applied the same principle. My daughter is a remarkable blend of beauty, intelligence, quiet strength, adventurous spirit, and unwavering dedication, with a keen sense of common sense. I never missed her practices, dance performances, cheerleading events, swimming classes, gymnastics meets, or any other adventure she embarked on. She forged her unique identity, drawing from her father's and my traits. Now, I am blessed with a granddaughter whose thoughts make my heartbeat.

My second son, born legally deaf and blind, embraced life to the fullest. Far from being reserved, he was incredibly sociable, engaging with everything and everyone wherever we went. I won't deny that it was both challenging and wonderful to witness. Every small milestone he achieved was a cause for celebration, and I continue to cherish these moments. He has pursued his passions, excelling as a musician and pursuing culinary studies. There are no limits for him. He ventured across the United States after falling in love with a bright, vibrant, beautiful young lady who shares his deaf blindness. They now reside together with their beloved cat.

My third child entered our lives during a period of great prosperity for our family. He embodies humor, rebellion, and boundless dreams, forever remaining my baby. Today, he thrives as a communication technical sound engineer, journeying across the United States alongside his team contributing to various projects.

However, the trajectory of my life was altered by ten years of legal battles in my divorce. My Husband left me when I received my PhD., was writing for a newspaper and had my own radio show.

My husband said he would clean his ass with my diplomas.

While in our divorce proceeding, he made my life so hard for ten years and was accused of fraud risking my integrity. While this was going on my son was undergoing chemotherapy. Due to the divorce my children and I lost our home. Attorneys kept it all plus what my ex had taken to another country.

This period not only consumed over a decade of my life but also impeded my mental wellness.

Yet, I choose to view those years of adversity as a catalyst for self-transformation.

My first two children are 16 months apart, and both were born while I was working on my master's degree. My second was born legally deaf blind. My third son was born in the middle of my doctorate. My ex-husband never visited me at any of my jobs.

Before marriage and while developing my career, my father didn't allow me to study abroad or out of state, nor did he support me financially, even refusing to fill out documents for student aid. My parents never attended any of my high school games. Two professors tried to persuade me to switch from psychology to social work. One wrote a sexist and racist letter when I applied to teach college. My mother prioritized me helping at home. As a Latina woman, I have faced many barriers from family, friends, and racist professors at the university I attended

I chose not to let life or others' opinions hold back my dreams. I realized I might not achieve my goals as quickly as I wanted since being a mom was just as important as my dream. I could please others by staying at home or changing careers and suppress my desires with thoughts like "I am not good enough" or "I wonder if I could have achieved my dreams." My choice had consequences. Eventually, my husband left, and people criticized me, attributing my achievements to my ex-husband.

Breaking Barriers: Navigating Entrepreneurship

As a first-time entrepreneur, my challenges included technology, business inception, platform development, forging connections, securing finances, and mastering sales. Plus, I had minimal support and faced inherited beliefs I didn't know existed within me.

How can I initiate my business venture? I sought guidance from my accountant, consulted Google, and Score, a nonprofit offering free mentorship for entrepreneurs. I followed their advice diligently, adhering to each step. Through this journey, I've realized the abundance of resources available.

Requesting help has always been challenging for me. Growing up, I handled everything independently, making it hard to admit I needed help. I felt inadequate and ashamed, facing judgment for my lack of tech knowledge. I reminisced about the confidence I felt organizing work on paper, effortlessly categorizing documents. As someone who thrived on physical movement, I found solace in pacing around the office, manipulating paperwork, and verbalizing my thoughts aloud. This method always seemed to work for me.

I struggle with computer skills, like building websites and managing social media. I'm grateful to my son Christian, and friends Theresa, Erika, Jennifer, and Paola, who helped me at little or no cost. Their support has been crucial to my progress. This journey taught me to overcome the fear of judgment and accept help, realizing that no business is ever done alone. Even small acts, like my friend Veronica introducing me to key individuals, have significantly impacted my business. Having someone listen to our journey, whether it's filled with achievements or sadness, can profoundly impact our lives. Their attentive presence validates our experiences and emotions, fostering understanding and acceptance. I would like to thank Graciela, Dennis, Walter, and Victor for reminding me that I was not alone.

So many times, I didn't want to face my biggest challenges. So, I found comfort in spending extra time on what I was good at and the business suffered. I learned that perfection isn't always attainable; what matters is taking consistent steps forward and being grateful for progress.

I learned to leverage my strengths and add value, I recognized that issues with sex/intimacy and money often cause relationship breakdowns. I co-authored the book "Let's Talk Sex and Money: Reinventing Conversations Among Couples" and contributed articles to "Latinas Con Poder" magazine on communication, sex, and intimacy. These efforts led to invitations for podcast interviews and eventually made me an international speaker. Before visiting new places, I connect with women's organizations to offer my services, realizing that ingenuity often matters more than money.

For me it does end by being in the public eye. Ongoing training from top experts in my field. I'm part of a group facilitated by Dr. Esther Perel, that supports coaches and psychologists. I undergo trauma training, read books by esteemed sex educators to enrich my expertise.

Another area where I delve deep is the realm of philosophy and healing modalities, particularly Tantra. I have participated "Institute of Authentic Tantra," which offers the only approved tantra training worldwide and presently with world known, Layla Martin.

What I remain committed to is staying at the forefront of my field. You see, coming from a culturally diverse society, my experience teaching cross-cultural studies and psychology has deepened my understanding and openness in interactions, especially culturally blended couples. My background in brain and behavior, along with ongoing mental health education, helps me recognize how conditions like ADHD affect communication, organization, sensory stimulation, and information processing in clients and their relationships. Gender differences are significant, but neither women nor men typically receive comprehensive sex education. Instead, societal norms often rely on pornography, locker room talk, or hushed conversations, placing undue responsibility on both genders to satisfy their partners. This neglects the importance of mutual understanding and accountability in fostering passion.

Life has surprised me in that my past experiences were preparing for this new life venture.

The Power of Authenticity and Connections.

Embarking on a business venture without financial backing may sound absurd, and there is certainly truth to that sentiment. Nearly everyone around me suggests that I should revert to my previous roles in the clinic or classroom and reserve weekends to nurture my business. However, running a solo enterprise demands significant time and dedication. I firmly believe that building a business from scratch is a full-time commitment. Consequently, I do odd jobs such as house cleaning, pet sitting, and house sitting to make ends meet. This lifestyle shift means preceding luxuries like dining out, socializing, and leisure activities like attending concerts or visiting my preferred gym. Instead, I prioritize essentials, preceding trendy clothes, and footwear to cover only basic expenses.

I yearn for those experiences, yet I find solace in the absence of these indulgences. Why? Because I have no money to start a business and the term "sales," I must confess it doesn't resonate. Realizing this, I acknowledged the need for coaching in this area. I delved into books like "Rich Dad and Poor Dad," but found them insufficient. My upbringing left me with profound unconscious neurological imprints that good people are poor and rich are bad. How absurd!

Being a psychologist, I know how this works. Our brain registers information in a story format. I formed this story of poverty and did not know how it drove my life automatically without awareness. Growing up, we often shopped at second-hand stores. My father would give me five dollars for clothes, only to criticize my choices, saying I could get more for less and reminding me of starving children in Africa. My mother remained silent, teaching us that heaven was for the less fortunate and fostering disdain for the wealthy.

These childhood experiences shaped our family dynamics. When my ex-husband and I reached financial success, my mother and siblings distanced themselves. Even sadder, when my mother was financially well-off, she hid her status, continued living as a victim, and never enjoyed her wealth.

Taking on my entrepreneurship made me face unhealthy unconscious beliefs I was unaware of. These old conversations still show themselves from moment to moment in my life.

Acting, observing the flow of my business, getting coached in the areas where I need support, and experiencing serendipities continuously remind me that "I got this."

How I see sales. That word does not work for me. It's a service where I accompany my clients on their journey to discover their path.

From couples ecstatically sharing they've experienced their best intimacy to women achieving their first orgasm, and from couples enhancing their communication to celebrating marriages and pregnancies – each success story fuels my passion. Some clients learn to navigate their attachment patterns, while others discover the importance of establishing boundaries or breaking free from unfulfilling relationships. Ultimately, authentic living infused with passion prevails, making every endeavor worthwhile. It's hard for me to see this as a mere sale.

Presently, abundance is on the making.

So, what keeps me going is why I so passionately believe in what I choose to do.

I believe it is my purpose for what I was meant to do.

Other Lessons Learned: Embracing Growth

I recognize and incorporate my past strengths into my journey while being willing to let go of outdated skills. Though some people may judge, their judgment reflects on them, not me. I expected support from some individuals but learned to let go of these expectations. Amid differing opinions, I trust my instincts, knowing that even a small step forward is progress.

One crucial lesson from books I've read is to learn from the best in your field. This has had a double impact: feeling that I'll never reach their level and realizing that aiming high means keeping an eye on top experts while reaching for the stars.

Networking takes time. Nobody knows you exist if you don't show up. I find every way to collaborate.

Financial restraints have been my biggest challenge. A nine to five job and creating my business didn't work for me. At my age, I had to choose between giving it my all or returning to my old career. I often felt like a lonely child watching others have fun. Being a solo entrepreneur is for no wimps. I found solace in podcasts by Wayne Dyer, Tony Robbins, and Les Brown. Now, Tony Robbins is endorsing this book, and I will train with Les Brown. Serendipity at its finest.

The Essence of Love: Passion, Purpose, and Transformation

As I sit here typing in Paris, my thoughts wander to the essence of love. For me, love is not just a fleeting emotion but the very fabric of existence, woven into life's tapestry. It is the image of my children and granddaughter, their smiles, sadness, and laughter like a melody in my mind. It is the warmth of my partner's embrace, the comfort of being heard and understood, and the bond shared with friends, siblings, clients, and strangers, united by our common humanity.

Love means feeling free to be myself and reflecting on those who've walked alongside me, whether through a smile, a negative thought, or a failed date that taught me something. Love is found in life's simple pleasures—a shared meal, the joy of laughter, the safety of a familiar embrace. It reveals itself in moments of connection and vulnerability. It's in music, dance, nature, and my erotic being.

The more I love myself, the greater my capacity to love others. To achieve this, I must embrace and transform my dark side. The greatest obstacle to love is within us—our stubborn insistence on being right, which hinders open and honest communication. Love alone isn't enough in a relationship; it requires partnership and a willingness to serve each other. Both partners must learn to resolve conflicts with humility and foster fun, connection, safety, and trust. Effective communication relies on listening and understanding. Building a partnership involves effort and learning to repair hurt. Love means surrendering to the unknown.

Yet, amidst love's beauty, a shadow exists—a darkness born of control and manipulation. In a society obsessed with goals, lovemaking has become an empty pursuit of pleasure, lacking passion and intimacy. Social media and pornography bombard us with images of fake couples, offering quick but superficial gratification, leaving us hollow and unfulfilled.

We suffer loneliness, starved of touch, kindness, and connection, relying on medication when our bodies can produce healing oxytocin naturally. Reflecting on my journey through love, I recall the pain of separation, heartbreak, and the lessons learned. Love requires patience, understanding, and forgiveness. Through love, we discover our true selves and find profound healing.

And so, as I sit here in Paris, surrounded by the hustle and bustle of life, I am filled with profound gratitude—for love, in all its forms, is the greatest gift we can ever receive. As long as we remain open to its infinite possibilities, we will continue to find beauty, joy, and fulfillment in the journey of love.

As I write this, I can't think of anything more beautiful. My work is meant to bring pleasure and love.

Conclusion: Embracing the Journey: A Love Letter to Life

Thus, like the tree which grows towards the sun, my story is still being written. I remain growing, learning, and inspiring people about what I love most, and nothing can hold me back. All the clients helped and consulted, all the workshops conducted, and all the written words fed the seeds of my purpose. And here, who can predict what new fruits will yield this tree? The idea that the journey itself is the destination is an excellent mantra that I intend to follow with respect.

Nowadays, I no longer operate as a solo entrepreneur. I've enlisted the assistance of an expert to manage social media, and I've also brought on board Paola, a youthful communication director well-versed in contemporary promotion and expansion strategies.

I serve clients from coast to coast in the United States and internationally. Additionally, I've expanded my reach as an International Speaker, and I'm currently penning this narrative from Paris.

Discover more about me and my various social media platforms by visiting https://linktr.ee/discoverpassionwithdrluz

For those interested in scheduling a sex and intimacy coaching session, book through my website at:

www.discoverpassionwithdrluz.com.

Should you seek a speaker for your event, please get in touch with me through my website.

Explore my latest book, "Let's Talk Sex and Money, -- Conversations to Reinvent Your Relationships" and delve into the initiatives of my nonprofit.

***

To contact Luz:

www.latinaswithpurpose.org.

Eric Lopkin

Eric Lopkin, a visionary entrepreneur and humanitarian, has left an indelible mark on the worlds of business and philanthropy. With a career spanning over 35 years across diverse sectors, including journalism, advertising, public relations, finance, medical research, and operations, Eric has amassed a wealth of multifaceted experience.

In 2009, driven by his passion for empowering individuals and organizations, Eric founded The Modern Observer Group, a trailblazing coaching and consulting firm. At its core lies a revolutionary system for Human Centered Achievement, which places individuals at the forefront of professional and personal success. Through his roles as founder and CEO, Eric has pioneered a culture of holistic success, prioritizing human well-being alongside business excellence.

Beyond his entrepreneurial endeavors, Eric serves as a beacon of compassion and service. He sits on the board of directors of several non-profits, including the CT Humane Society, which advocates for animal welfare, and The Support Info-Go Initiative, which connects individuals with ongoing medical conditions to vital support groups and resources.

An accomplished author, business coach, podcaster, and speaker, Eric Lopkin continues to leverage his profound insights to uplift and empower others, leaving an enduring legacy of positive impact and transformation.

Success Starts with Taking Care of People

By Eric Lopkin

We live in a rapidly changing world. Artificial intelligence, virtual work, economic challenges, and more must be considered when planning for success. Even with changes coming fast and furious, a person is still at the core of success. Measuring success in terms of productivity or financial metrics is no longer enough. We must also measure the impact of what we do on ourselves and the people who rely on us and our businesses. Achievement is not just about reaching goals but about doing so with mindfulness, compassion, and a holistic approach to life. The human factor is the key. This is Human-Centered Achievement (HCA). When using HCA, success is not simply about getting things done. It is about getting more of the right things done with less effort and less stress. Focusing on people, whether that means taking care of your employees, customers, team, or yourself, creates an environment of success in all aspects of life. Beyond work-life balance, this level of success is work-life integration. To succeed in work and life, you must be able to manage your health and stress and be in the proper mindset to achieve peak performance. The basics of doing this include mindset, focus, time management, process creation, and evaluation.

Mindset is the basis of all perception. It consists of how you view yourself and the world. It is also the most common cause of failure. Your mindset defines who you are. Are you arrogant or modest? Are you active or passive? How do you perceive things?

Mindsets are beliefs—beliefs about yourself, your abilities, and the world around you. Your mindset determines how you view your skills, intelligence, and talents. It determines your personality and how you view others.

People with a fixed mindset believe that what is, cannot be changed. This leads people to avoid challenges they do not think they are capable of because they do not want to be embarrassed by what they believe is a failure that cannot be avoided. By contrast, people with a growth mindset enjoy challenges despite the risk. This is because people with a growth mindset are confident, they can continue learning and developing new skills. They feel that even if they do not have a capability at the moment, that can be changed as they learn and grow.

To embrace Human Centered Achievement, you need to develop a growth mindset. Accept that you are not perfect and do not need to be. Everyone has flaws and quirks. They are part of what makes you unique, which is a good thing. No one thing defines you, and you can change and adapt. Embrace change and push yourself to improve. While you are not perfect, that does not mean you should be satisfied with the status quo. Keep exploring, keep learning, and continue to improve.

You should also focus on having a positive attitude. No matter what challenge is in front of you, you can face it. It may take more work than you expect but be willing to put in that effort. When you have negative thoughts, acknowledge that you had the thought, but also acknowledge that it is not necessarily true. We all have moments of doubt, but do not let those moments control your actions. When others express doubt, accept that it is their opinion, then prove them wrong. Remember, it is not necessary for you to succeed immediately. Allow for the time needed to accomplish what you want. Taking ownership of your mindset and actions is also very important. Accept that you are responsible for the choices you make and the impact of those choices.

The mindset of HCA prioritizes human needs and values. It involves cultivating self-awareness, resilience, and a growth mindset. Instead of focusing solely on outcomes, individuals embrace the journey, learning from failures and celebrating progress. Adopting a positive and empowering mindset enables individuals to navigate challenges with grace and determination.

Mindset is just the beginning. To truly succeed, action is required. HCA emphasizes the power of focused attention. It involves identifying priorities, setting clear goals, and dedicating time and energy to meaningful tasks. Individuals can achieve greater productivity and effectiveness in their endeavors by minimizing distractions and honing in on what truly matters.

This focus is necessary for effective time management. No one truly manages time; you simply use it efficiently. By understanding one's energy levels, identifying peak productivity periods, and allocating time accordingly, you achieve your goals while minimizing stress.

Once you have identified when you work best, you need to identify your priorities. You must be able to distinguish between tasks that contribute to long-term goals and those that are merely urgent but not important. By focusing on high-impact activities and delegating or eliminating low-value tasks, individuals can channel their efforts toward what truly matters, leading to greater fulfillment and success.

After you track when you work best and decide on your priorities, you need to create processes to complete your tasks. The key to a successful process is simplification. You don't want to have to figure out how to perform a task every time you have to. The best processes make tasks simple, allow you to maintain high quality, and remove stress from the task.

While we think of processes in terms of work, you also need to create them for the rest of your life. We always do this, although we tend to think of them as routines rather than processes. A morning routine, a recipe for your favorite meal, a date night ritual, and a workout are all types of processes. Incorporating these life processes can increase your health and reduce stress. As stated earlier, HCA is about holistic success. To succeed in work, you need to succeed in other areas of your life.

When you put together processes, whether for your life or business, they do not have to be complicated. For most processes, a simple checklist is all that is needed. Break down tasks to their simplest steps and write them down. You have a process. For more complicated work, consider using a flowchart. This will allow you to follow along and take different results into account.

In an organization, processes also serve another function. You don't want each person in your business doing the same job in a different way. You must create processes and document them so that as new people join the organization, they know the proper way to do things. This ensures that no matter who in your organization is servicing your customers, they get the same consistent, top-quality experience, and your employees and team members can reduce their stress levels.

Have you been in a franchised restaurant lately? Wherever you are, when you walk into a restaurant that is part of a franchise, you know what to expect. There may be regional variations, but in general, the food is the same, the decor is the same, and the service is the same. The people, however, are not. Even though the people running each restaurant may never have met, they are consistent, if not identical. This is the franchise system. Each owner gets a manual that explains how to do everything step by step. The franchise owner follows the directions, and the franchised business runs. Now, think of your business as a franchise. You need to create processes that make your business run smoothly. You want to be able to replicate what you do, even if you are not there. If your business cannot run without you, you can never take a vacation or get sick because the business would stop. You may decide to sell the business one day. If the business can't run without you, the value is zero. Processes are the difference between a business and a job.

You want to make each function possible to be handled by the lowest possible level of skill. Every process should be broken down into the simplest possible steps, but don't leave anything out. Even though you are trying to make things easy to run, it is crucial that everything gets done. The goal is to produce extraordinary results with ordinary resources and people.

Even with the focus on simplicity, your processes must be able to adapt. They must integrate feedback from employees, customers, suppliers, etc. They must remain flexible while still guaranteeing the same or better results. The whole point of the process is to make things easier and more productive.

Once you have set your growth mindset and accepted that you can always improve, and you have figured out what tasks you need to do, when, and how to do them, you must check your work. Regular reflection and evaluation are essential aspects of HCA. It involves assessing progress, identifying areas for improvement, and celebrating achievements. By embracing a continuous learning and growth feedback loop, individuals can refine their strategies, overcome obstacles, and stay aligned with their values and aspirations. As stated earlier, this is not simply about financial metrics and achieving goals; it is also about assessing how you and others affected by the work are reacting. Are you relaxed or stressed out? Are you focusing on business and ignoring the rest of your life? You must define what needs are important to you and the people you work with and determine if you are fulfilling those needs.

HCA is facilitated by the creation of intentional processes. It involves designing workflows, systems, and routines that support productivity, well-being, and work-life integration. By establishing rituals for self-care, boundaries for rest, and frameworks for collaboration, individuals can cultivate sustainable habits that promote success and fulfillment in all aspects of life.

Once you have mastered the basics, you start seeing benefits, whether you are implementing the system for yourself or your business. The benefits to a person from HCA are fairly obvious. Businesses can also reap numerous benefits from embracing HCA principles within their organizational culture and operations.

By prioritizing the holistic well-being of employees, businesses can create a positive work environment that fosters engagement, satisfaction, and loyalty. When employees feel supported in managing their workloads, balancing responsibilities, and maintaining personal wellness, they are more likely to perform at their best and contribute meaningfully to the organization.

Your people are a strategic advantage. Employees are an opportunity. They are thinking, idea-generating, and responsibility-taking assets. Most people are far more attracted by hope, optimism, and freedom than by negativism and restriction. If you truly expect to benefit from a person or team's best effort, each person needs to sense that you have faith that they can and will deliver.

HCA encourages individuals to focus on high-impact tasks, manage their time effectively, and optimize their energy levels. As a result, employees become more productive and efficient in their work, leading to better outcomes and greater success for the business.

By promoting open communication, mutual respect, and collaboration, HCA fosters a culture of trust and transparency within teams. This facilitates smoother workflows, better decision-making processes, and stronger relationships among colleagues, ultimately driving innovation and problem-solving.

Businesses prioritizing HCA are more likely to attract top talent and retain valuable employees. When individuals feel valued, supported, and empowered to achieve their personal and professional goals within the organization, they are more inclined to stay long-term and contribute to the company's success.

HCA encourages a growth mindset and a willingness to learn from failures and setbacks. This mindset fosters adaptability and resilience within the organization, enabling teams to navigate challenges, embrace change, and capitalize on new opportunities more effectively.

Companies prioritizing human-centered values and practices tend to build stronger relationships with customers, partners, and the community. By demonstrating a commitment to the well-being of their employees and stakeholders, businesses can enhance their reputation, attract loyal customers, and differentiate themselves in the marketplace.

In essence, HCA benefits individual employees by promoting well-being and fulfillment and leads to tangible business outcomes such as increased productivity, better collaboration, and enhanced reputation, ultimately driving long-term success and sustainability for the organization.

Human-Centered Achievement also means meeting the human needs of your customers. How can you deliver outstanding customer service above and beyond the norm? You need to exceed your customer expectations, but you need to do it while keeping prices competitive. Customer service has gotten so bad at many companies that standing out in this field is not difficult, but you must make the effort.

When you decide how to serve your customers best, let yourself be guided by your experience with customer service. You don't need a complicated analysis to know when you have received poor customer service. Expectations of customer service are affected by the price of your product or service. The higher the price, the higher the expectation. People think you get what you pay for. As a business owner, your job is to give them more than they pay for. Provide the customer service that you would want if you were your customer.

If a customer says you met their expectations, it's easy to assume that you did a good job. But what if the customer had low expectations? You need to set realistic customer expectations and then exceed them—preferably in unexpected and helpful ways. To set customer expectations realistically, your whole organization must be involved. From product development to marketing, all aspects of the business must work to project and protect your brand image.

Offer great value and provide a clean, stylish environment for customers. Empower your front-line employees—everyone who works with customers. Surpassing expectations on the service side means that you, your suppliers, and your employees understand what your brand stands for and are proud to be associated with it. This means you have to appreciate and engage the people who work with you. Unhappy workers will never be able to fake good customer service.

To maximize the benefits of HCA, it is useful to understand yourself and your organization. This starts with your core beliefs. Take time to discover why you are doing what you do. When you understand your own core beliefs, you can create an organization that focuses on them. Organizations operate on a limited number of core beliefs and assumptions ingrained into the business's very fabric. To build an organization that has truly engaged employees, consider its purpose.

When determining your organization's common purpose, permit all stakeholders (managers, employees, owners, and customers) to benefit, each in their own way. Recognize that, regardless of the endeavor, each stakeholder wants to know what they are getting out of a situation. Until you satisfactorily address that question, you can't unleash the full potential of what can be accomplished.

Think of all your stakeholders as members. Winning organizations recognize that membership is a privilege. The foundation of every smart recruiting process or marketing campaign is that membership has privileges and is not for everyone. Your job is to find others with common beliefs who share your beliefs and passions with those of your organization. Never deceive or take advantage of stakeholders.

If the company conducts its business in a satisfactory way to the people who work there, most employees will excel.

Looking at success from a holistic point of view, taking into consideration the sometimes-conflicting needs of business, life, and career demands is the key to real, lasting success. Achieving your goals and getting more done while reducing stress and increasing enjoyment for yourself and others spreads success and increases well-being.

***

To contact Eric:

To learn more about how you can benefit from Human Centered Achievement, go to https://modernobserver.com, schedule a Zoom call with Eric Lopkin at https://modernobserver.com/schedule-a-call or call 203-693-4523 x101.

Andrew Hurst

My name is Andrew Hurst. I am a certified life coach from Dothan, AL. I have a BS in Interdisciplinary Studies concentrating in philosophy, promotion, and leadership from Troy University. I also have multiple certifications from iPEC Coaching, including Certified Professional Coach(CPC),Energy Leadership Index-Master Practitioner (ELI-MP), and Core Dynamics Transitions Specialist (CDTS).

I have a passion for learning and developing myself, and I enjoy traveling, video games, music, art, science, psychology and philosophy. I believe that everyone has the power within them to create positive change in their life, and I would love to see you shine on your own journey. Upon hearing about Jim Britt and "Cracking the Rich Code" I knew this would be a great opportunity for me to share coaching expertise with the world. This community of coaches, consultants, CEO's and business leaders has given me knowledge and insight into a world of entrepreneurship that has empowered me to write my section of the book. When you read "Cracking the Rich Code" it is my honor to present you with best practices from my work and to be included among the contributions of professionals in this book. When you read this book, let it challenge, inspire, and educate you on the many ways to be rich. My hope is that you come away from this book with renewed passion, interest, and excitement to achieve your own personal and professional endeavors.

The Coaching Process

By Andrew Hurst

What is a coach? Is it someone you go to for advice? Is it another kind of therapy or counseling? These are all relevant questions people have when you tell them you are a life coach. Coaching is partnering with clients in a thought provoking and creative process that inspires them to maximize their personal and professional potential. This work is often misunderstood as therapy and counseling because while it does incorporate some of the same verbiage and techniques it is more focused on satisfying the clients present needs and wants to then collaborate on the best strategy to move forward. As a coach it is my job to make sure that what the client is telling me is aligned with their personal values, professional ambitions, and spiritual walk. When I sense that their story is making them discouraged, stressed, and overwhelmed it becomes my duty to observe, challenge, and investigate those claims and see how it reflects upon the mirror of their true self. Over the course of our time together it is my pleasure to see people go from 0 to 10 on their levels of self-confidence, self-discipline, personal growth, maturity, and integrity on their journey to self-mastery. One of the hidden perks of working with a coach is that you end up getting more value than you thought was possible. This starts to become obvious when the client begins to realize that the problem they thought they had was actually a limiting belief, assumption, interpretation, or fear of their situation or themselves. My goal as a coach is to provide guidance, reflection, introspection, and context in their struggles. The magic of coaching starts by giving people the space to be themselves without facing judgment or criticism. There have been multiple studies on the benefits of letting the client lead the conversation and the coach to act as the facilitator. In my experience as a life coach thus far I would add that coaching is the process of creating space for self-discovery for the client that helps them grow and transform their personal and professional life. Giving someone the opportunity to be themselves and tell their story in a coaching relationship is one of the best acts of service you can do for someone who is seeking change and hope in their life. When the space is available for the client to share their thoughts and feelings on a topic that is important to them, they are more likely to respect and appreciate the coach's feedback. From the perspective of the client this makes them feel seen and heard in their present situation. As the conversation progresses, the coach will be able to gather information on the clients fears and concerns as well as begin to see the pain points, internal conflict, and external influences that seem to be blocking their overall happiness and well-being. One of the key skills that coaches bring to the conversation is the ability to drill deep into the pains, worries, stresses, and fears of the client for the coach to get a holistic look into their psyche. Once questions are raised about their core beliefs, emotions, and reactions to the problem they are facing, then the conversation shifts to what the client wants to believe, think, and feel about the situation. This part of the process is where the client starts to see the light at the end of the tunnel and begins to choose new and empowering beliefs, thoughts, and feelings to help them overcome and find peace with their struggles. The coach's role here is to facilitate this part of the conversation until the client is ready to fully embrace this new paradigm they have created for themselves. As you can see the coach acts as the advocate, cheerleader, and mentor of the client's journey to fulfillment and success. Today, there are many people in need of a coach and they don't even realize it. If you or someone you know has ever wondered 'Who do I need to become to get x outcome or result?' Then seeing a coach would be in your best interest. The practice of coaching is best suited for those who want to create goal-oriented and task-focused solutions tailored to one's individual mission. Those who look at the prospect of coaching with skepticism and scrutiny are those who most likely don't believe in themselves. Here are three reasons why people may resist coaching.

1. They are unwilling to face change
2. They are afraid of feeling uncomfortable
3. They are afraid of being held accountable

Some people fear being coached because they know it is going to bring up areas in their life where they need to make changes. Whether the coaching they receive is personal or professional, the goal is to improve performance and that means one must be willing to change their beliefs and actions in some area of life. If they don't believe that change is necessary, then they don't believe they need coaching. However, that notion is incorrect. The very best performers in every human endeavor work with coaches on some level. Their core belief is that if they change something, they can perform at an even higher level. Once a critic of coaching sees evidence of this empowering belief, they will be challenged to take this topic seriously and start to see the potential benefits of what coaching can do for them. Even though human nature is naturally selfish, there are two sides to one's self-interest; one side feeds the ego while the other side feeds the self. In psychology the terms Ego and Self represent the dual sides of one's persona. The Ego represents the desire for strength, justification, ambition, achievement, and attention. The Self represents the desire for love, joy, peace, freedom, and enlightenment. The coaching process addresses both sides of the persona that paves the way for the client to obtain inner peace and reconciliation. The best coaches touch the heart, stir the spirit, and free the mind. Humans are hard-wired to act in alignment with self-identity. To rise above your personal story, one must have the courage to venture into the unknown. Coaching ultimately sheds light on these four life lessons: Happiness is the new rich. Inner peace is the new success. Health is the new wealth. Kindness is the new cool.

Coaching Myths

Every successful person you can think of has sought out the wisdom, insight, and practical guidance of a coach when they needed a shoulder to lean on, someone to hear them out during a hard time, or someone who would help them in a time of great uncertainty. When people see what coaching is all about there will be no more confusion and speculation about this work. As the coaching industry has evolved over the last forty years it is just now coming into mainstream thought and consideration. In today's culture it has become evident that people are looking for unconventional solutions to modern day issues. Additionally, people today are looking for ways to lighten their load, relieve their stress, and seek answers to questions that have eluded them for years. Coaching can provide solutions to all these concerns and more to those who are willing to be teachable, reasonable, and proactive. Part of the magic throughout the coaching relationship is witnessing the client gain self-awareness, self- discipline, and self-confidence to achieve anything they want. When people hear about coaching but never receive any coaching, they are likely to make some assumptions and interpretations that don't accurately reflect the intention and mission of this work. Here are some common myths about coaching:

1. Life coaching is the same as therapy
2. Life coaching is only for people who have problems
3. Life coaching is a one size fits all solution
4. Life coaching is expensive and time consuming
5. Life coaching is easy, and anyone can do it
6. Life coaching is a fad and not a serious profession

If you or anyone you know has believed or stated any of these myths, please help them understand that all of those points are coming from ignorance and confusion. Again, coaching is about helping clients find solutions to their own problems in a thought-provoking and creative process. Now let's debunk these myths and shed light on the truth of the matter.

#1. Life coaching is the same as therapy. People are trying to make a connection between a therapist's role of diagnosing an issue combined with the motivation you get from a sports coach. While this assumption is someone wanting to define this term for themselves, it is a problem because it obfuscates the intention of coaching. If I heard someone tell me this, I would politely inform them that the difference between coaching and therapy is the former is about hearing the client's current situation and then help them create a path forward to personal and professional success. The latter is about hearing the client's story of personal trauma and mistreatment and allowing them to vent their frustrations to eventually diagnose the problem with the help of medication.

#2. Life coaching is only for people who have problems. This is a misunderstanding of what coaching is meant to fully accomplish. While it is designed to tackle problems it can also be used for less serious concerns by asking questions like: What do you want to talk about today? What are your top three priorities right now? What do you want to change about your current situation? What are some thoughts you have when things are not going your way? What are some small steps you can take today to get closer to your goal? All these questions are applicable to virtually every conversation you could have with a client. At the beginning of the coaching conversation the coach is supposed to open the floor for the client to set the topic and tone for the session. What questions open up the mind to explore and introspect on what are the most important topics for discussion.

#3. Life coaching is a one-size fits all solution. This point is completely false. Any honest coach would tell you that every client's solution is unique to them, and processes information differently based on their experience, mindset, and belief system. If this point had any truth to it, then everyone would want to seek a coach and the industry would be treated like a fast-food business. Alas, that is not the reality of this business and certainly not the goal of good coaching. What people might be projecting in this statement is 'Why can't everyone just be more like me?' which is a poor attitude to take on the subject because the average person is a collection of societal, communal, familial, and personal conditioning. If you wanted to break those chains, you would probably seek out a professional because you can't make all those changes on your own. In fact, if someone were to do all this inner work by themselves they will get stressed, overwhelmed, and miserable after beating their head against the wall so many times.

#4. Life coaching is expensive and time-consuming. Unlike the other points so far this one is understandable. What people are afraid of is doing their diligence to find a coach that is right for them, pay a subscription or premium, and participate only to feel that you are not getting anywhere with the investment. Unfortunately, this situation has occurred too often by fake coaches who are more interested in selling online courses just to make some money but leaves the individual feeling stranded and frustrated. The way to combat this injustice is for the buyer to look for offers that include 1-on-1 coaching for at least two months and have some information on how the coach will inspire, encourage, and hold the client accountable. If there is no mention of these values in their marketing material that is a red flag for anyone looking for an honorable coach.

#5. Life coaching is easy, and anyone can do it. This is quite an overconfident remark from skeptics. It is not easy work, nor can anyone do it because being a coach is both an art and a science. At its heart, coaching is about bringing your most humane qualities forward and helping others to see the inherent value, beauty, and strength in their humanity as well. People are meant to think, feel, and act more purposefully while working with a coach. It takes a special person to fully appreciate and realize the kind of service, dedication, and attention a coach can bring to someone's life. What people might be thinking here is 'I think it's easy to get into coaching so I can call myself a life coach and sell whatever I want.' While the coaching industry is mostly unregulated today that does not mean you should market yourself as a coach that can solve people's problems. That kind of attitude will ultimately ruin any chance you have at gaining respect and admiration from a potential audience when your offer has no substance.

#6 Life coaching is a fad and not a serious profession. Out of all the myths I have found, this one is the most ridiculous. Coaching is an honorable profession because in order to be a respectable coach you need to show that you have people skills, interpersonal skills, communication skills, listening skills, emotional intelligence, honesty, integrity, and authenticity. If people were honest with themselves, they don't possess all those skills hence why they would seek a coach who could help lead, guide, and direct them to awaken their potential and cultivate those skills in their own life. It is not a fad because people are now looking for ways to gain clarity, insight, and direction for their life in a busy and crazy world. As life gets more chaotic, people are struggling to find balance and purpose. A coach simply helps you realize a fulfilling and harmonious life faster and easier than you thought was possible.

Coaching and Leadership

One of the hidden opportunities that coaches have today is to be a voice of wisdom in a world that is drowning in a sea of information. I believe that coaches have the power to influence society in a positive direction to help others recognize the need for compassion, collaboration, and competence. As a life coach, it is my honor, duty and belief to serve clients with their best interest in mind. My vision is aligned to helping clients achieve breakthroughs and find meaning in their personal and professional lives. My mission is to provide knowledge, insight, understanding, and empathy when discussing strategies, challenges, and goals on the path to success. My passion is to guide clients to awaken potential and make purposeful decisions that align with their life goals and aspirations. Today the world is looking for new leadership. People that will push us beyond the status quo and create a world that is equitable, wonderful, and productive. Our ability to change is directly related to our intelligence. When you place someone's IQ, EQ, and SQ together you get a full picture of someone's abilities and potential. (Intelligence Quotient, Emotional Intelligence Quotient, and Spiritual Intelligence Quotient). I say this because this is one of the frameworks I have adopted to gauge a client's overall potential. The average of these three measurements gives the coach a greater understanding of the client's potential. This is a tool that monitors overall progress throughout the client's journey of personal growth, emotional maturity, and spiritual evolution. One of the skills that can be cultivated through the coaching process is the dormant leadership skills in the client. Most people don't realize they have leadership skills because they have never been in a position where they have had to act as a leader. Interestingly, leadership and followership are two sides of the same coin. If one is a good follower, then they have an idea of what it takes to be a good leader. Coaches can demonstrate leadership skills by instilling confidence, persistence, and resilience in the client as they go about their journey of transformation. Successful leaders also make for great coaches. There is an overlap of skills between these two titles because both are geared toward identifying outcomes and helping people achieve those outcomes by focusing on their strengths or upskilling their weaknesses. Coaches and Leaders also see that communication and comprehension is paramount to achieving personal and professional success. Whether it be 1-on1 or team settings, both professions champion communication that enable the clients and teammates to be treated as equals when sharing difficult topics and sensitive situations. Working with individuals to identify their strengths, weaknesses, and aspirations, coaches and leaders can help create a roadmap for success and provide the support and guidance needed to achieve goals. Coaches who act as leaders want every client to succeed and surpass their original expectations. The relationship among coaches and leaders also lends itself to fostering better understanding, trust, and care within discussions. When a client's energy and enthusiasm becomes open to expansion, that's when the authentic self-starts to emerge. This part of the coaching relationship is truly fascinating because that is where the coach and the client bring out the best in each other. It is a symbiotic relationship between facilitator and participator. As the core energy of the client rises, so does their ability to see the road that leads to happiness and fulfillment. The role for the coach starts to take a spiritual turn as the road to self-mastery becomes the awakening of one's higher consciousness. The Self starts to arise to create balance and harmony within the client. It also puts the Ego in check by transforming it into a more mature, reasonable, and courageous version of what it used to be. Ultimately, Coaching and Leadership can be used together to make further progress in the life of the client and provide hope to those who are seeking answers to life's toughest questions. A coach sees the invisible, feels the intangible, and achieves the impossible with you.

***

To contact Andrew:

ahurst909@gmail.com

334-790-8841

LinkedIn: Andrew Hurst Level Up Coaching

Jennifer Brown

Jennifer Brown's career exemplifies exceptional leadership and unwavering social responsibility. Leveraging her psychology background (Cal State Los Angeles) from impactful work in special education, she transitioned to real estate, where she has thrived for the past 25 years.

Jennifer's expertise extends beyond the real estate deal itself, encompassing strategic planning for acquisitions, development, and investments.

A visionary leader, Jennifer's impact extends beyond the boardroom, and her commitment to making a difference is further exemplified. Holding leadership roles in real estate, mortgage, and non-profits, she champions women in business as the First Vice President (two terms) of the Women's Council of Realtors, Los Angeles. Her dedication extends to the Southland Regional Association of Realtors, where she delivered the 2022 invocation speech.

As a business consultant and entrepreneur, with her diverse experience and unwavering commitment to gender equality, she empowers and inspires business owners.

In 2018, she founded Embrace Charitable Foundation, a testament to her philanthropic efforts and leadership outside of the professional sphere. The foundation empowers foster youth and serves the community through education and financial independence initiatives, and she mobilized volunteers to feed over 2,000 families in need.

Jennifer Brown is a force to be reckoned with, shaping the future of small business owners, while leaving a lasting, positive impact on her community

From Stuck to Soaring: Unleash Your Potential

By: Jennifer Brown

I have learned so many lessons throughout my life, and it is difficult to know where to start. Lately, I've been reflecting on this wild ride, all the twists and turns, the "oh no!" moments, and the "YES!" breakthroughs. It's a treasure trove of lessons learned, social molds I happily shattered (and some I'm still chipping away at!), struggles that tested my grit, and triumphs that still make me do a happy dance.

But the kicker? There's a whole bunch of stuff I wish I had known back then, so I could have faced those challenges with wide-eyed wonder (and maybe a little less stress!). So, I figured, why not share the wisdom and maybe a few laughs along the way with you?

Ever feel like you were constantly being cast in other people's plays, throughout life?

Yeah, me too. Growing up, I spent a lot of time on introspective walks, dissecting my choices, feelings, and the company I kept. Now, with hindsight's 20/20 vision, I see the molds people tried to squeeze me into – some supportive, some downright suffocating. It makes me wonder, were you always the star of your own show, or did you ever feel like you were playing a part written by someone else? I'd love to hear your story too!

My mom, bless her heart, was a champion lock-downer. If helicopter parenting was an Olympic sport, she'd have a gold medal. Of course, this just fueled my inner escape artist – I became a master at finding loopholes and forging my own path.

My childhood stomping grounds were a fascinating mix. Picture a giant apartment complex, a self-contained universe with its own social orbit. Every age group knew each other, playgrounds buzzed with activity, and evenings were spent stargazing on blankets spread in the greenery. Apparently, that "universe" was actually called "housing projects." The funny thing is, it never felt like poverty to me. My mom, a dedicated nurse, just needed a little rental assistance. We weren't rich, but we weren't struggling either. The neighborhood had its rough patches, but there was a strong sense of community, a feeling of safety woven into the fabric of the place.

And the labels? Oh, the labels! "Spoiled brat," "pushover," "goody-two-shoes," "lazy bum," "failure," "stubborn," "outsider." Quite the collection, wouldn't you say?

The thing is, none of those labels defined me. And now, they're just echoes from the past. Back then, I was riddled with self-doubt—afraid of rejection, failure, and colleagues' judgments. Facing those fears was like staring down a lava pit—daunting but necessary.

I had to learn to embrace my imperfections, forgive myself for stumbles, and celebrate what made me unique.

Growing up comfortably middle-class, my parents preached the gospel of the college degree. So, I did the "right" thing, got my bachelor's in psychology, and promptly... well, promptly didn't find success. The degree collecting dust on the shelf wasn't exactly the financial windfall I'd envisioned. Job hopping became my reality and my first foray into business with partners. Let's just say it was a learning experience (epic fail).

Have you ever felt like success is a team sport, but finding the right teammates is harder than finding a unicorn? Yeah, me too.

Early on, I craved the camaraderie of achieving things together, but I quickly realized it takes a special kind of crew to truly win as a team. Building that dream team? That's a whole other ball game.

Discouraged but not defeated, I struck out on my own in real estate. I climbed the ladder, from residential clients to commercial ventures, but along the way, I lost myself. The people, the pressure, the grind – it just wasn't a good fit. One day, I slammed on the brakes. This rat race wasn't getting me anywhere.

It was time for a reboot. I deconstructed myself, identified the areas I craved change, and visualized the person I wanted to be. Honesty became my guide. I accepted my truths and learned to filter life's experiences, letting go of negativity and embracing all that empowered and inspired me.

Here's the thing: I'm not some extraordinary wonder woman. I'm just an ordinary person who craves more out of life, someone who thrives on helping others blossom. That's the core of my business – a service built on my passions and fueled by learning and growth.

Sometimes, people don't see their potential in themselves, or they lack the purpose and vision to fan those flames. But hey, guess what? It's never too late to learn and grow. Our minds, hearts, and souls are ageless repositories of wisdom, constantly evolving despite the wrinkles on our suits (as my dad, "forever young at heart", would say!).

Life throws curveballs, that's a given. But when adversity strikes, humor is my secret weapon. Sure, it's okay to acknowledge your feelings – wallow for a minute, even! But don't get stuck in that emotional jacuzzi. Jump into the cold pool of self-awareness, find the humor in the situation, and move forward.

Every setback holds a lesson. It's about learning from the experience, dusting yourself off, and taking that knowledge into the next round. Because there will ALWAYS be a next round, with its share of highs and lows. Don't let life pass you by. Break free from the routine's hypnotic rhythm and embrace the ever-changing melody of life. After all, time is a river, and we're all just floating on it. So, paddle hard, embrace the twists and turns, and make the most of this incredible journey!

Success? It was always a moving target. Amazing ideas are like butterflies, fluttering just out of reach. But that's the beauty of it! Complacency is my kryptonite, and the chase keeps me on my toes.

This is just a glimpse into my story, and guess what? It's still being written, and you're invited to join me. Let's break free from the mold and rewrite our own narratives, one life chapter at a time.

Do you ever wish you had access to a treasure trove of life lessons at your beck and call, just begging to be shared with you whenever you feel lost?

You're not alone. This journey called life throws a curveball (or two!), and sometimes, the biggest growth comes from the "what if," and then we turn them into "let's do's."

Here's a big truth: Fear can paralyze you. It whispers doubts, holding you hostage in your comfort zone. But what if we reframed the question that we tend to ask ourselves? Instead of "should I?" ask, "What's the worst that can happen?" Often, our initial fears are wildly overblown.

This simple shift empowered me to take the leap —to embrace the unknown and chase my dreams. It wasn't always sunshine and rainbows. There were failures, like my first business venture. But through it all, I learned that the most valuable lessons are often the hardest ones.

Here are some golden nuggets I've unearthed:

- **Self-discovery is key:** We all have a unique path. Avoid being afraid to break free from societal molds and embrace what truly sparks your soul.
- **Redefine success:** It's not a one-size-fits-all. Define what success means to YOU. Is it financial freedom, helping others, or a fulfilling career?
- **Embrace lifelong learning:** We never stop growing. Open your mind, seek knowledge, and watch your potential soar.
- **Mindset matters:** Your perception shapes your reality. Cultivate a positive outlook, and watch obstacles transform into opportunities.

Remember, it does not matter where you are in life or what stage you are in. You can always restart over. Just as the moon sets, there is a new day in the sunrise. This is just the beginning of your journey. Let's ditch the status quo and embark on your journey, one powerful lesson at a time. Let's crack open the secrets to personal and professional growth, untangling the key points that can unlock a whole new level of you.

While I can't share every lesson I learned in this single chapter, I can offer four powerful key points that I hope will empower you. These learnings shaped me and challenged me.

Let's dive in!

Key Point #1: The Partner Trap: Why Going Solo Can Be the Smart Choice

Have you ever dreamt of starting a business with friends? Think about it. The energy, the camaraderie – it sounds amazing, right? But hold on a sec. Before you jump into that entrepreneurial adventure with your BFFs, let's talk about something crucial: choosing the right partner.

Because here's the truth: the wrong partner can turn your dream into a nightmare. Disagreements erupt, frustration builds, and suddenly that exciting venture feels more like a sinking ship.

Why? It's all about alignment.

Think of a business partnership as a marriage. You need **absolute trust**, a shared vision, and the emotional intelligence to communicate openly and honestly – even when it's tough. Both partners need to be willing to receive constructive criticism with grace because growth requires open minds.

Now, imagine your partner forgetting what was agreed upon months ago. Frustrating, right? That's why **ironclad agreements** are essential, no matter the partnership type. A written document, clear and signed, protects everyone in the long run.

So, what if you haven't found that perfect partner?

Don't despair! Here's a powerful truth: sometimes, going solo is the stronger choice. It allows you to build the **right team** around you, a team that complements your strengths and propels your vision forward.

Remember, incredible people are out there, ready to join your journey. You just need to find the ones who fit the puzzle, not force a square peg into a round hole.

Here's something to ponder: Is the temporary comfort of a familiar face worth the risk of jeopardizing your dream?

Choose wisely, because your business's future depends on it. There's strength in numbers, but there's also power in a clear vision and the right team by your side.

Key Point #2: Unleash Your Inner Leader: The Ripple Effect of Transformation

Do you ever wonder what the secret sauce of successful companies is? The answer might surprise you: it's leadership—strong, visionary leadership that inspires, motivates, and empowers people to achieve incredible things.

But leadership isn't just for CEOs and top dogs. It's a skill we can all cultivate, no matter our title or position. **Think of it as a ripple effect.** Your actions, your decisions, your energy – they all impact those around you. The question is, what kind of ripple are you creating?

Here's the truth: effective leadership is a journey, not a destination. It requires constant learning, growth, and a willingness to adapt.

So, what makes a Transformational Leader?

Imagine leaders like Eleanor Roosevelt, Martin Luther King Jr., or Nelson Mandela. They possessed a powerful combination of traits:

- **Vision:** They saw a better future and inspired others to believe in it.
- **Empathy:** They understood their people's needs and connected with them on a deeper level.
- **Courage:** They weren't afraid to take risks and stand up for what they believed in.
- **Action:** They didn't just talk the talk – they walked the walk.

These aren't mystical powers – they're learnable skills. Here are some ways to start your leadership journey:

- **Invest in yourself:** Read books, attend workshops, and seek out mentors.
- **Embrace lifelong learning:** Stay curious and open-minded, and always seek new knowledge.
- **Practice empathy:** Listen actively, understand people's perspectives, and build genuine connections.
- **Lead by example:** Your actions speak louder than words. Be the change you wish to see.
- **Empower others:** Give your team the tools and resources they need to succeed. Celebrate their wins and encourage growth.

Remember, leadership is a gift. When you choose to lead with purpose and authenticity, you create a ripple effect of transformation— not just in your own life but also in the lives of those around you.

Are you ready to make a difference? The journey starts now.

Key Point #3: Level Up Your Circle: Attract Success Like a Magnet

Ever feel stuck on the success ladder, yearning for that next rung? You're not alone. But the truth is, achieving your dreams often hinges on who you surround yourself with.

Imagine a vibrant network: a community of people who have climbed mountains, solved puzzles, and emerged stronger. These are the go-getters, the ones who inspire you to think outside the box and conquer any challenge. They operate on a higher frequency, their energy fueling your own drive and creativity.

These are your power players! They'll not only challenge you to be your best, but also connect you with others who can add rocket fuel to your business.

But beware of the energy drainers. Those negative Nellies are the ones who haven't walked your path or built their own empires. Their whispers of doubt can be toxic, hindering your progress and zapping your mental well-being.

Here's the key: curate your circle with intention. Seek out mentors, friends, and influencers who are on a similar trajectory and who radiate positivity and growth.

Think of it this way: surrounding yourself with successful people is CONTAGIOUS. Their experiences become your steppingstones, and their insights become your roadmap.

Build bridges, not walls. Networking isn't just about what you can get; it's about building genuine connections. When you connect with others and offer value, amazing things can happen. You never know who might become your next champion, amplifying your success and propelling you even further.

And let's not forget your dream team! Building a strong team of professionals is crucial for any business to thrive. Here's your A-team roster:

- **The Legal Eagle:** An attorney who acts as your business bodyguard, helping you navigate potential pitfalls and keep you legally sound.
- **The Money Maestro:** A CPA who empowers you to understand your finances, maximize tax benefits, and keep more money flowing back into your business.
- **The Market Mavens:** A Realtor® and/or stockbroker who stays ahead of the curve, offering you the best options and expert guidance for your investments.
- **The Growth Guru:** A business consultant who helps you identify the growth levers that will propel your business to the next level.

Remember, the right connections are invaluable assets. By surrounding yourself with these power players, you'll not only climb the success ladder faster, but also create a network that amplifies your impact and fuels your journey to the top.

So, who will you choose to elevate your circle? The choice is yours. But remember, the company you keep truly shapes your destiny.

Key point #4: Unlock Your Business Potential: Goal Setting and Time Mastery

Ever feel like your business dreams are stuck in first gear? You're not alone. Many entrepreneurs get caught in the whirlwind of daily tasks, losing sight of the big picture.

But here's the secret weapon: clear goal setting and effective time management.

Imagine this: you have a roadmap to success. It answers the critical questions that will guide your journey:

- **What is your "why"?** What is your business's purpose? Who are you impacting?
- **Who are your power players?** How are you different from the competition?
- **What's your financial vision?** What kind of revenue goals do you have for yourself and your business?

These are the building blocks. Once you have a clear picture of your destination, it's time to break it down into achievable milestones.

Here's the trap to avoid: Staring at that mountain of a goal and feeling overwhelmed.

The solution? Chunking! Break down your long-term goals into smaller, manageable phases. This way, you can focus your energy and avoid procrastination.

Think of it like climbing a mountain:

- **Phase I: Research & Discovery (Time Frame: XX weeks)** This is your base camp. Here, you gather intel on your competition, costs, and the tools you'll need.
- **Phase II: Implementation (Time Frame: XX weeks)** Now you're scaling the mountain! You assemble your team, determine your operating space, and refine your tools.
- **Phase III: Working on the Business (Ongoing)** You've reached the peak! Here, you analyze your first quarter, learn from the experience, and set new goals for continuous improvement.

Remember, every successful journey starts with a single step. By setting clear goals and managing your time strategically, you'll transform your business dreams into a thriving reality.

Conquer Your Goals! Avoid being stuck in the mud and become a Mountain Master!

Feeling stuck can be a real drag, like your business wheels are just spinning in the mud. It happens to everyone. But by chunking your goals into manageable phases, you've created traction and pushed yourself forward.

Now you've navigated the phases, climbed the mountain (metaphorically, of course!), and planted your flag at the peak. Now what?

Now, take a moment to savor that incredible feeling of accomplishment. You've achieved a major milestone, and that deserves a high five!

Here's the thing: things don't always go according to the perfect plan. Life throws curveballs, deadlines get nudged, and that's okay! Be kind to yourself. If you need to extend a phase, do it. It's your climb, and you get to set the pace.

And remember, there's no shame in asking for help. You'd be surprised how many people are willing to lend a hand. Your network is a treasure trove of support, so don't hesitate to tap into it.

So, what are you waiting for? Grab your metaphorical climbing gear and start building your roadmap to success!

Thank you for spending some time with me on this chapter. I truly believe it's just the beginning. As you turn this final page, **Remember:** the fire to achieve your dreams already burns brightly within you. Avoid being afraid to fan those flames into a blazing inferno. Believe in yourself and in your potential and chase those dreams with reckless abandon. The world needs your unique spark, and I can't wait to see you out there, shining brilliantly with the success you so richly deserve. Go forth and conquer!

***

To contact Jennifer:

https://jennybrealtor.com

https://embracecf.org

Email: Jennyb@et-precision.com

Tanya Steele

Tanya Steele is a professional trainer, safety advisor, and co-host of the *Safety Debris* podcast. As an expert in health & safety committee training, she helps both business owners and their teams understand and implement safety in the workplace. She's known as the First Lady of Safety because her training is renowned across the country for being just as fun as they are informative and effective to ensure that Safety Makes Sense™ – every day!

Tanya is on a mission to improve people's quality of life, daily – especially on Mondays! Why Mondays, you ask? Research shows that more workplace injuries occur on that day than on any other weekday. That's why it's so important to have a safety program that is easy to understand and implement. Her company delivers in-person and virtual training, using a wide variety of techniques to transform safety into dynamic and engaging experiences so leaders can Work with Confidence™, deepen their purpose, and increase production – all while having fun!

She's been interviewed for several news publications and has co-authored several books. Over the years she has held board positions, including Regional VP of the Canadian Society of Safety Engineering, President of Safety & Health Week (NAOSH), and the President of the Canadian Association of Professional Speakers (BC chapter). She recently received "Top Women in Safety" award through the Canadian Occupational Safety magazine.

Rivers of Service:
A Journey of True Wealth

By Tanya Steele

I like making money as much as the next person. However, I've learned that being rich is not just having wealth and material goods. Living a rich life means finding fulfillment, true joy, happiness, and gratitude. Only then can "being rich" genuinely feel rich.

People occasionally ask me, "What is the secret to your success?" The title of this book puts another spin on that question: what is the secret to "cracking the rich code?" Since starting my business in my mid-20s, I have always had the same reply: "Serving."

From as far back as I can remember, my parents taught me the importance of living a life of service. My mom was a caterer and an amazing host, so I learned how to serve guests when they came to the house. Likewise, if an opportunity came up to volunteer in the community, we jumped at it. When my family started going to church, we volunteered in different areas—even cleaning toilets. Someone had to do it. Why not us?

In my late 20s and early 30s, I wanted to make a difference in our world by serving overseas. So, when Venezuela suffered a devastating flood in 1999 that killed tens of thousands of people, I applied to be part of an emergency medical team. Thanks to my paramedic background, I was accepted to join 9 doctors and nurses who were travelling from around North America. Let me tell you the secret of "cracking the rich code" that I learned on that trip.

Our mission was to bring medical help and supplies to Venezuelan families who were living on piles of dirt where their houses used to stand. There was no clean water, no power, and no shelter since the flood had washed it away. As we drove through the neighbourhoods of Los Corales, Cerro Grande, and Carmen de Uria, our brains could not process what we were seeing. Mud and debris filled people's houses. People were literally sitting on the roofs of their homes because they couldn't go inside. All along the street, cars were buried, trees knocked over, and boats piled up on top of each other. It was truly the most devastating thing I had ever seen.

We spent the first few days in a larger city. From the start, our days were full: we distributed bandages, wrapped strains and sprains, splinted minor fractures, cleaned infected wounds, and handed out medication to help with the pain or treat the parasites we could see moving under children's skin.

We were asked to go into a remote village and help a group of people that lived in the jungle. We instantly agreed to this request and started making the arrangements. However, I had no idea what we signed up for.

We woke up early on our travel day so we could go to the river and travel to our destination before it was too hot. The government had just issued a heat advisory, telling everyone to stay indoors between noon and 3 PM due to dangerously high temperatures. As we made our way to the river, my brain was making a list to ensure our safety: "Drink lots of water. Stay covered up. Stay out of the sun." I took comfort in the fact that we were starting early, before the heat of the day.

At 6 AM, we arrived at the location where we had arranged to meet our guide and boat. As you can imagine, communication was a little bit of a challenge due to the language barrier. However, we were confident that our guide was on their way. After two hours of waiting, sitting beside the river, we felt a little less confident. Following up with our hosts, we were assured that the boat was on its way. We simply had to wait a little bit longer. "No problem," I thought. "It's only 8 AM. We still have several hours before we have to stay indoors. Once we're on the boat, we will just stay under the shelter of its roof."

As I waited, I decided to talk to a young girl who was fishing at the side of the river. She was maybe seven or eight years old and had caught several fish. Curious, I peered into her little bucket. The fish were small, a little bit on the flat side, and maybe 4-5 inches at their widest part. Yet, their faces and mouths looked a little odd and unfamiliar. I commented to the little girl that she was doing a great job fishing and then asked her what kind of fish she was catching. "Piranhas," she replied nonchalantly. Alarmed, I jerked back. I didn't want to have my fingers too close to the bucket. And then it dawned on me that this river that we were about to travel on was full of piranhas. This day just got a little more unpredictable.

11 AM eventually rolled around, and there was still no boat. The temperature was on the rise, and we were starting to get quite warm standing on the river's edge. However, once again, we were assured that the boat was on its way. Our boat arrived right at high-noon, peak temperature, a fact that made my safety brain begin to tilt.

To make matters worse, the boat wasn't what we expected. The best way I can describe it is to say that it was a steel dugout in the shape of a canoe. It was powered by a small motor—the kind that you might use if you were fishing on a small lake. What's more, it had no roof or cover or seats. It was wide enough in the middle to hold three plastic folding chairs. So, we were able to put two rows of three chairs in the middle of the boat and everyone else had to lie down in the bottom of the boat.

I don't know what we would have done if we were tourists. Thankfully, our hearts were open to serve. We tapped into our ability to be flexible, got in the boat, and started making our way down the river.

As we slowly moved along, we had lots of time to look at the surroundings. The poverty of the scene was striking. Small houses, perhaps better described as huts, sat on either side of the river. They were made of metal sheets and mud. At various intervals we could see children walking on the side of the river in shorts, no shirts, and bare feet, carrying sticks or playing with rocks.

The river's edge also had more alarming inhabitants: namely, a concerningly large number of alligators. When I commented on them, the boat guide casually told us that alligators take more lives than any other animal in the area. At one point we saw a cow carcass floating in the river beside our steel dugout. In response, the guide explained that it was common for alligators to grab cows that wandered too close to the river's edge. Once a cow was floundering in the water, it would be surrounded and devoured by swarms of piranhas.

Conscious of the heat and the need to look after our bodies, I asked our guide where we could pull over to take a break and maybe use a restroom. He looked at me like I was from another planet. We were not stopping, he declared: we did not have time. If we needed to go the bathroom, we just had to drop our drawers and plunk our butt over the boat's edge. As you can imagine, this revelation prompted us to make some difficult decisions about our voyage. For the women in the group, myself included we made the dangerous decision to stop drinking water. None of us could imagine ourselves peeing in front of our colleagues.

So, to recap, we were floating on a steel dugout, with no cover, in a river full of alligators and piranhas. Worse, we were travelling in the hottest part of the day—on a day when we had been advised to stay indoors because of extreme heat. And to top it all off, we stopped drinking water so we wouldn't have to go to the washroom. My safety brain was beyond frazzled and beside itself.

After several hours had passed, a miracle happened: our boat guide decided to pull over to the side of the river where a family was waving at us. We were so grateful to get off the river, even for just a few minutes. The older lady of the group looked to be the mom of the three young children standing beside her. Two of the children eagerly approached us, smiling from ear to ear, while the youngest clung to her leg, wary of these strangers who were disembarking from the boat.

Hurriedly greeting the family, we asked if there was a washroom nearby. The mom pointed around the back of the house. Relieved, all of us girls smiled, said thank you, and started towards the back of the house. However, when we arrived at the back, we discovered that there wasn't even an outhouse. Just acres of mud and jungle. We did not want to wander too far from the house itself because we were not sure of what we might encounter inside the jungle area. So, we all looked at each other and then lined up along the back of the house, squatting down to do our business, sharing a single roll of toilet paper that made its way from one end of the line to the other.

Somewhat refreshed, we returned to the family, whose excitement at our presence had not faded one bit. They invited us into their home, and we gratefully accepted—anything to prolong this rest stop! The house was rustic, to say the least: mud floor, mud counters, and some steel sheeting for its walls and roof. Their beds were hammocks tied either to a tree or to the side of the mud walls. For water, the family had created a filter system out of a bucket with holes and some sand. When they poured river water through the sand, it would filter out whatever larger chunks were floating in the water.

This family had very little, but their generosity was larger than anyone's I had ever seen in my entire life. The children, although covered in dirt and ragged clothes, seemed happier than my neighbours' kids who have so much more. The kids grabbed our hands and showed us their chickens. They smiled and giggled when one of our doctors did a little magic trick with a coin. To our surprise, their mother—through some broken English, hand signals and eyes full of love—insisted that we stay for dinner. She had killed one of her chickens and was currently boiling it with the intention of serving it to us—all to express her gratitude that we took the time to stop by.

Sure, our doctors gave her and her children a medical checkup. We also left her with some bandages, some clothing, and a few other personal items that we thought might be helpful. Yet, what we gave them was nothing compared to what they shared with us. They had seen this boat of strangers who were overheated, fatigued, and hungry. In response, they served us, helped us, encouraged us, and even sacrificed two or three days of food to feed us. What an experience of unconditional love and kindness. She and her family were our hero's that day!

As we resumed our journey, we all sat in silence for quite a while, each of us reflecting on the family's generosity, grateful for the food, enriched in spirit. I think this was the moment that the true definition of "service" began to take shape in my life.

The remainder of our trip—which lasted until after midnight—continued to be eventful. The sun set, unleashing unthinkably dense clouds of mosquitoes and Jurassic Park-sized dragonflies that feasted on these smaller insects. By now it was pitch black, the kind of black that is so dark that you cannot see your hand in front of your face. Suddenly, a mysterious something thumped hard against the boat. The guide immediately turned off the motor. It felt like we all stopped breathing. A dead silence engulfed us. Even though I couldn't see a thing, I instinctively looked down to see or feel if water was starting to come in. Were we about to become piranha food?

The guide turned on the only light we had, a small double AA battery flashlight, and started looking around. The fear was palpable. My mind was racing. *What if the boat starts to sink? Do we jump out of the boat? What if half of us went to one side of the river and the other half went to the other side of the river? Then what?* I could hear my heart pounding in my chest. I felt helpless. I had no idea what to do, except to sit and wait and see.

As a first responder, "wait and see" was not in my vocabulary. It felt like an eternity went by, knowing that no one was coming to our rescue anytime soon. But the guide eventually finished his inspection. When we asked what had thumped into us, he just shrugged and restarted the motor. On the outside, he at least, seemed unfazed and unbothered: for him, it was just another night journey on the river!

We survived it all and eventually made it to our village destination. While I was laying in my hammock that night, I evaluated some of my core beliefs. Why did I need to be the rescuer? Why was I so terrified that I could not save us from the danger, when just a few hours earlier a miracle happened with a stranger that took us in when we were in need? She gave us everything we needed with her sacrifice. Why lose the faith only a few hours later?

So, why have I bothered telling you this story? What does it have to do with how I've run my businesses, let alone "cracking the rich code"?

For starters, I learned what true service looks like. It's easy to think that "service" is an extra, something we offer as a luxury. In some ways that's what I thought I was doing when I signed up to go to Venezuela. However, that riverside family taught me otherwise. Service takes sacrifice. I thought I was there to serve them, but they took great delight in serving me—and served me in self-sacrificially generous ways that still bring tears to my eyes. Their example gave me deeper compassion for people and the ability to receive from others who want to help, support me, or speak into my life.

For all three of my businesses, I have learned to ask for help or accept help when it is offered. Instead of beating myself up, I am now grateful for these moments when there is nothing I can do, and I have to rely on others.

Moreover, true service is not dependent on ideal circumstances. In my story, nothing went the way it was supposed to go, sometimes, like in business. The boat was late, the river was filled with dangers, and the traveling conditions weren't just uncomfortable—they were borderline unsafe. And yet, those circumstances were a gift. I am not saying to do things unsafe in your business, but thanks to this experience, I learned that it is okay to do things scared. You just need a little faith and perseverance, and you will get where you need to go. I also learned to embrace the failures, make the necessary changes that will grow my company stronger. It may not always look the way you thought it would, but if you are committed to the outcome, you can make it happen.

Today, I continue to prioritize volunteer service in my life. I'm more strategic about where I serve—I spend time in associations whose members are my ideal clients. As well as a few community, non-profit organizations, that I believe in. It also helps me build relationships with others that I can collaborate with, ask questions of, and personally help them in the same way. Some of my largest clients are people I met while serving and volunteering.

When one of my company's hit its first million dollars, I immediately thought of that day travelling in the steel dugout and how that experience helped shaped my career. My business continues to reap the rewards of those lessons.

Even my day-to-day work is dependent on this service principle. For example, before starting my health & safety committee courses, I take a moment to remind myself why I'm there. No matter how I feel that day—energetic, tired, lackluster, or blah—I am there to serve and give everything I can in that moment. I'm there to help my clients promote practices and systems that preserve lives. Reminding myself that I am there to serve helps me stay focused, and it also helps me turn something like safety legislation into an experience that's fun, engaging, and practical. The kind of experience that equips people to Work with Confidence™ because they know and believe that Safety Makes Sense™.

My goal, every day, is to set up my clients and staff for success by finding ways to serve each of them. That's why I open every meeting with a simple question: "How can I serve you today?" I want to understand what metaphorical rivers they're traveling down so I can give them what they may need, in that moment, to keep going.

With that goal, honouring the gifts of service that I received, I strive to be someone's hero every day. And if you ask me, that's what "being rich" looks like.

***

To contact Tanya:

https://johsc.ca/home/

Diane Smyers

Diane Smyers is a business leader and passionate advocate for empowering those facing adversity. As a former foster youth, she intimately understands the challenges of envisioning a brighter future beyond one's circumstances. The guidance of mentors and a court-appointed advocate during her time in foster care was pivotal, helping her recognize her potential and the limitless possibilities that lay ahead.

Smyers' remarkable career spans influential roles at organizations like The Walt Disney Company and Google. In 2023, Smyers was named "California Woman of the Year Making HerStory" by Assemblymember Freddie Rodriguez 53rd District and "Woman of the Year" by the City of Upland. In 2024, she received the "California's 40 Women over 40 Making a Social Impact Award" for her exceptional contributions to empowering foster youth and calling her community to action.

A dynamic speaker, consultant, coach, and author, Diane leads by example, demonstrating how to overcome past adversities and create a future of one's own design. She founded Inspiring Warriors, an organization dedicated to empowering individuals to dream beyond their current situations. Her remarkable achievements, bold spirit, unwavering commitment to social responsibility and genuine passion for fostering positive change, stands as a beacon of hope, empowering individuals to envision and actively pursue their dreams, regardless of their circumstances.

Unconditional Love
Compassion Interrupted

By Diane Smyers

Growing up, I always felt different - an outsider, even among my family. "Do you love me?" I would ask my parents, desperate for reassurance that never resonated deep within. The words rang hollow against the emotional neglect and violation of trust I endured at the hands of my father from as young as three years old. I was just an object to him, not his daughter. This wound burrowed into my heart, leaving me grasping for value and belonging that seemed to elude my grasp for decades to come.

At school, I could drift between social circles - the popular crowd, the party crowd, the athletes, and smart kids - but authentic connections remained elusive. I kept my distance, never fitting in. I was active in sports (and good at it.) But, often told to withdraw from the sports, I loved to be home to serve a dictator who felt "a woman's place was to serve him.". I was an odd child doing anything to get attention. I was eluding everyone on the surface, concealing the heavy secrets and self-doubt that weighed me down. "Would anyone miss me if I died?" "Would they notice if I cut my wrists?" (The answer is no, they didn't notice.) The darkness crept in, whispering that I didn't matter.

How does a child find the words to ask their parents, "Do you love me?" It was a burden no child should ever have to bear. It's painful to think of even today. It was my reality. Soon, my reality of loneliness and isolation was about to intensify. The announcement of our family's sudden move from sunny Southern California to a tiny Colorado town disrupted what little semblance of normalcy remained in my turbulent life. In a dizzying blur, I found myself uprooted from everything and everyone I knew - my social circle erased, my grandparents, aunts, uncles, cousins – gone! My entire world flipped upside down with only a day's notice. I was ill-equipped to process this fresh upheaval as a teenager. I had no time to prepare for a significant life change. With a one-day notice, I frantically flew around my high school to collect signatures, contacts, and my version of "well-wishes" typically shared in a yearbook. There was no time for that formality.

I dropped into the unfamiliar halls of my new school, and I stuck out like a sore thumb. The slow, quiet pace was a harsh contrast to the liveliness of my hometown and school. The culture shock was undisputed for this California girl. Nicknames came like lightning bolts, such as "Valley Girl" and "Rich B****," rained down as I struggled to find my footing. Loneliness and isolation enveloped me. Why couldn't I live in California with my grandparents, aunts, or uncles? The only answer echoed by my father was, "We don't want to split up the family." It was foreign to me since my brothers lived in other states or cities, nowhere close to us. The family was already split up. God was about to intervene in a big way.

Little did I know, God was quietly guiding me toward strangers who would show me the meaning of unconditional love and forever transform my trajectory in life. My life was about to be interrupted by the compassion of strangers who would grow to feel like family.

My high school counselor, Jody, was the first to extend a warm welcome and reassuring presence. I was drawn to her office repeatedly, our conversations deepening into shared prayers, talks about Jesus, and an ineffable sense that she perceived something "off" about my situation. On April 11th, I walked into Jody's office for my daily dose of prayer and encouragement. Words I could never fully own tumbled out: "My dad hurts me, and I need help."

It wasn't me speaking - it was some wiser, braver essence welling up to shatter the deception I had been conditioned to uphold. At that moment, Jody's unconditional love enveloped me like the hug that followed. She listened, letting me know she was obligated to report what I had disclosed, but reassured me that everything would be okay. For the first time, I knew what it felt like to be genuinely heard, valued, and loved unconditionally. I don't envy the phone call she had to make and the subsequent confrontation she had to face with my parents.

April 12th is seared into my memory - the day my fragile world fragmented before my eyes. Summoned to the principal's office, I was met by grim-faced officers and a social worker with a sickening revelation: my home situation had been deemed unsafe, and I was being taken into the state foster care system immediately.

The humiliation of being publicly paraded down the hallways, a cautionary tale for my classmates to gawk at, is something I can never forget. Tears and shame burned my cheeks as I was ushered outside like a criminal and deposited into the back of a police car. Just like that, my grasp on any sense of a normal childhood was violently ripped away. I soon realized my "normal childhood" was not normal at all.

I spent that first night on a cot in the social worker's office, adrift after the traumatic upheaval. Yet, human connections that would soon change my life were waiting in the wings. Unconditional love had been preparing to catch me throughout my freefall into the unknowns of the foster care system.

Placed with the Redman's, a foster family in Colorado Springs, I plunged into a fresh nightmare where food was strictly rationed and locked away. Then, one night, in a shattering instant, my foster brother David came home drunk, high, and carrying a loaded gun. I watched in horror as he shot himself in front of us. His anguish over being one credit short of graduating and a school's unwillingness to allow him to walk in the graduation ceremony a day away got the better of him. The friends in his life did him no favors by allowing him to return home in such a suicidal state without notifying the Redman's was horrifying.

Amid the anguish, shock, and secondary trauma, I found the strength to call my former pastor in California for help. As a retired Los Angeles County Sheriff, I followed his advice, requesting I be moved to a faith-based emancipation home. I then reached out to Jody, my steadfast ally, who came to my aid.

Jody was a supportive presence at my high school graduation the next day. Graduation seemed surreal for many reasons. I attended this school less than 21 days prior to graduation. The night prior my foster brother attempted to kill himself and the family. My grandparents and four-year-old nephew were in the stadium with my parents; however, I never saw them, I was committed to keeping the family's secrets as to why I was living thirty miles away from my parents. This trip by train was the last trip my grandmother ever made.

With the gunshot still ringing in my ears, I was appointed a Guardian ad litem (GAL) volunteer named Virginia, who would become another critical figure to throw me a lifeline of unconditional love. She did not see my behavior as a problem. She saw ME! She saw the possibilities within me. Often, after being emancipated from the foster care system at 17, I would go to her law firm, assisting her with files, talking about boys, and her taking time to help me see I could become anything I wanted. The only limits I had – were those I self-imposed.

Looking back, those tumultuous years in foster care hold crystal clear moments when human compassion and unconditional love pierced through the darkness like a beacon in the storm. Jody and Virginia saw my potential vividly, even when I could not. Their tenacious advocacy ensured I received the critical services needed and the nurturing of strengths that allowed me to heal, rebuild my fractured self-worth, and ultimately thrive.

This pair of steadfast and loving supporters were not required to remain in my life, champion my future, or fill the hollow void where family failed me, yet they did. They showed their belief in me with selfless constancy and unconditional love. They loved me when I couldn't love myself. With each reassurance and personal investment, they chipped away at the learned limitations I had internalized as an embattled foster youth.

Mentored by Jody and Virginia's unconditional love and care, I began daring to dream bigger than daily survival—envisioning stability, self-sufficiency, and the ability to positively impact the world. Those visions seemed fanciful for a child conditioned to temporary circumstances and upheaval. But their commitment kindled an ember of hope, allowing me to see myself as a successful entrepreneur and supporting me on a path to turn dreams into my living legacy.

As the years passed, the relentless tenacity that allowed me to endure the foster care system's turbulence transformed from a survival tool into a powerful asset for professional perseverance. With guidance, that persistence propelled me to build a business from the ground up

- becoming living proof that foster youth can achieve remarkable heights when supported by compassionate, tenacious, and unconditional love.

The very qualities and mindsets that helped me navigate the trauma of childhood gave rise to an authentic leadership style rooted in resilience and realness. I found myself supporting others in my life with the type of unconditional love shown to me. Like those who embrace their imperfections as sources of wisdom, honoring their truth above projecting a superficial facade, I learned to lead with vulnerability and transparency. With a kind heart, fierce mind, and a brave spirit of unconditional love for anyone who crosses my path, I became a judgment-free zone for hurting people.

My life came full circle the day I joined a CASA (Court Appointed Special Advocate) program that once uplifted me from my darkest valleys. A new chapter opened with a sense of profound purpose. I had the opportunity to serve as a CASA volunteer myself, being that presence and source of unconditional love for a foster youth walking through their foster care journey today, being a victim of human trafficking by multiple pimps. Being on staff for a CASA program empowers one child at a time, much like Jody and Virginia did for me through their unconditional love and support. Their belief catalyzed a ripple effect, allowing me to reimagine the heights foster youth can reach when surrounded by a commitment to advocacy and loving them through their valley while championing their successes. If you could imagine throwing a pebble into a lake, the ripple effect forever changes the lake. It is no longer the same. Unconditional love is powerful and life changing.

This journey had clearly been composed by a great God, with both triumphs and afflictions purposefully woven into the tapestry of my destiny. Along the way, an indelible truth became illuminated – "I was born for such a time as this." I was born to share my unconditional love with other foster youth, to give hope and a voice, and to champion foster youth in my community, my state, and nationwide. I am the beacon of unconditional love, a voice for change, healing, and inspiration.

For me, that grand choreography coalesced when I stepped into my role as a voice and fierce advocate for the foster youth community I once belonged to. Converging through the clockwork were the leadership abilities tempered by years of resilience, an authentic realness shaped by personal experiences, and an intuitive empathy born from having walked in their shoes.

In those full-circle moments, we transcend from a chapter of personal turmoil into the opening overture of a greater contribution to the world's song. No longer are we recipients of circumstance but co-creators guided by purpose. This is my pain-to-purpose story.

For so long, the weight of my past traumas and struggles in the foster care system felt like shackles holding me back from fully embracing life. The psychological scars of being unwanted, moving from home to home, and dealing with abuse within the foster care system left indelible marks. Try as I might to move forward, I carried those wounds deep within me everywhere I went.

Even as I slowly carved out independence and stability as a young adult, I remained haunted by the ghosts of my past. My constant companions were anger, sadness, confusion, and feelings of unworthiness. I struggled with attachment issues, finding it hard to cultivate deep connections or trust others. Subconsciously, I think part of me felt I didn't deserve true happiness and belonging after being discarded and mistreated so many times throughout my youth.

It took years before I realized just how much baggage from my turbulent upbringing I had allowed to weigh me down. My past may have shaped who I was, but it didn't have to define my present or determine my future. Clinging to the resentment, the pain, the cycles of self-doubt, none of it was serving me. If anything, it was only compounding the trauma instead of finally allowing those wounds to heal.

The process of forgiving myself and others and letting go of that immense emotional burden was not easy. It meant confronting demons and memories I had suppressed. I was a master at disassociation, not allowing myself to feel the depths of pain and rejection I experienced as a child. Through therapy, journaling, and tapping into my inner strength that has gotten me through the toughest of times, I slowly started to chisel away at the emotional shackles binding me to the past.

With each step towards forgiving the family who abandoned me, the abusive foster parents, the sexual assault while in a group home, and the cyclical brokenness of the system, I felt layers upon layers of weight leaving my soul. Hatred, anger, sadness - those insidious feelings that had cemented themselves within my psyche started to loosen their grip. In their place blossomed self-acceptance, inner peace, and a profound sense of freedom and possibility for my life.

Forgiving does not erase the past or make the deep hurts magically disappear. There is no obliteration of the struggles and hardships that mold our experiences. But it does upgrade us from imprisonment, chained to the past and all its devastations. When we can take that essential step towards forgiving ourselves and others, we cut the anchors holding us stuck in trauma for far too long.

My past will forever be part of my journey, but it is no longer a heavy yoke I carry. The more I was able to forgive, the more light filtered into my life. The more hope I had. The bigger the smile on my face. The more unconditional love I could give to others. I broke through cycles of self-destructive behavior, depressive moods, and feeling unworthy of love and happiness that had plagued me for so long. There is incredible power and peace in no longer being accountable to the shackles of the past.

It will always be part of shaping me into who I am today - an empathetic, resilient, strong-willed, and unbreakable warrior. But it no longer holds me hostage. I decide my fate now, not my former traumas. We all could shed those weighty shackles that have held us back for far too long. Forgiving sets us free.

One final step I came face to face with was forgiving my parents and healing the hurts of a young three-year-old unprotected child that was victimized for 13 years. I never quite got to full forgiveness with my father before his passing.

I walked through the journey with my mother, drawing closer to her with each honest conversation and each admission. God allowed me to see (truly see her) and hear her heart. Her final two years of life were the most honest, healing, and restorative of our relationship by her admission and apologies for failing to protect me from a predator. She freed me to tell my story, as messy and complicated as it is. My mother admitted her childhood abuse, and, in some way, we walked a journey of healing childhood traumas together. I supported my mom with the same level of unconditional love and compassion shown to me for decades by Jody and Virginia. Often, they didn't want to hear the details of the abuse I endured – yet they listened. I was able to be that for my mother and watch decades of secrets fall from her face and shoulders. Releasing the shame she carried – even though the shame was not hers to carry. She carried secrets for nearly 85 years. When she passed away, she did so, knowing she no longer (we no longer) had to carry the burden of childhood secrets and traumas. Her smile was more authentic and softer, and I believe she was met by the truest form of unconditional love the day she entered Heaven. She (we) was free to live.

Abuse and neglect victims must be met with compassion, grace, and unconditional love. As a person committed to "Loving people through their healing," I can say that extending grace and allowing others to be heard is life changing. God equipped me to offer unconditional love amid the most difficult of stories. I don't know who I'd be today if I hadn't been interrupted by compassion.

Serving foster youth and victims of abuse, neglect, human trafficking, and more is my calling in life. I proudly stand as a limitless example of possibilities when victims are heard and loved, and healing is championed.

While I can pinpoint many of God's fingerprints along my journey through the foster care system and the impact of those connections- My life's trajectory was interrupted by compassion in Colorado by a kind-hearted high school counselor, a former Pastor from California, a Court Guardian-ad-litem (GAL), and met by the most impactful of all, the eventual unconditional love of my mother.

***

To contact Diane:

Or for your next retreat, event or conference go to

Diane@inspiringwarriors.co

or call (909)560-2788.

Dr. Mindy Gewirtz

Mindy Gewirtz is the founder and president of Collaborative Networks International a leadership and executive coaching firm. Dr. Mindy is an executive and leadership success coach, best-selling author, speaker, and entrepreneur. She partners with leaders to level up their leadership skills and behaviors to get a future fit for success and promotion. The result is often individual, team, or organizational transformation. Mindy's global clients include healthcare, high-tech, biotech, alternative energy, manufacturing, government, and nonprofits.

Mindy, a Master Certified Coach (MCC) is accredited by the International Coach Federation (ICF) and the (EMCC Global) European Mentor and Coaching Council. Mindy's Ph.D. was earned at Boston University. An Adjunct Faculty at Lewis University for several years, Mindy taught *Coaching Methodology* and *Coaching/Mentoring* courses in the Master of Organizational Leadership (MOL) program. Mindy mentors US, India, Saudi Arabia, and Germany coaches applying for MCC accreditation. A Board-Certified Diplomate (BCD) and licensed psychotherapist in Boston, she was also an adjunct faculty at Boston University.

Mindy co-authored the book, Conversation Secrets for Tomorrow's Leaders: 21 Obvious Secrets Leaders Do Not Use Enough, 2021. Mindy's chapter in her coauthored book Cracking the Rich Code: How to be Rich in any Area of Your Life with Jim Britt and Kevin Harrington, Volume 11, 2023 focused on Worklife Adaptability. She also wrote five other book chapters on leadership, teaming, and managing change. Mindy and her husband plan on celebrating their next big anniversary by tandem skydiving.

7 Leadership Secrets for Living a Life That Works: The Adaptive Framework

By Mindy Gewirtz

"I don't want roses," I cried, hot tears running down my face. "I need help!"

I took the bouquet of a dozen, long-stemmed roses that were offered. My rational brain understood the gesture as a peace offering for the previous night's unresolved argument. I felt like smashing the roses on the shag carpet where we were standing, but I knew I would have to clean up the mess. Instead, I took the bouquet and shoved it in the garbage can in the kitchen, crushing the delicate petals.

The argument that begat the roses incident decades ago was my decision to go full-time to graduate school after I had won a full two-year scholarship, although my partner and I agreed I would go part-time for four years. I must say with five children in tow under the age of seven, two twins, going full-time was more than a little crazy.

This is my work/life-origin story. It reflects my missteps and pain in balancing conflicting life and work/career interests. Yet, this incident precisely triggered cracking the rich code of a lifelong passion for making a difference as a change catalyst in people's lives, teams, and organizations. Whether as a therapist, an executive, an organizational consultant, or a leadership coach, I found time to speak, coach, research and write about the dilemma of integrating life and work. Reflecting forward, learning has always been my means of coping, and I needed a lot of it.

I have witnessed and wrestled with the evolution of work/life balance, from close-up. Caring for the family was seen as a woman's total responsibility through the 1950s. Even when more partners began to help in the 1960s and 1970s men were considered exceptional when they helped a lot. The man who left work early to attend his son's soccer game in the 1970s and 1980s received accolades. A woman who did this was on the "mommy track." This term was pejorative. It meant a woman wasn't serious about her career and no longer was on the fast track for promotion.

In the 1980s-1990s, organizations began recognizing how the work/life dilemma impacted engagement and productivity for women and a new generation of men. Progressive organizations began building childcare centers on-site or provided voucher services for daycare in the community. I experienced the sputtering false starts of this arrangement with a famous textile company, Malden Mills, Inc. when I was consulting, coaching, training, and proposing an onsite childcare center, dependent care vouchers, etc. -- until a fire broke out and the childcare project went up in flames. Some organizations offered bounded flexibility opportunities which meant coming early to work and ending early to create the space to care for children or elderly family members. But very few had flexibility during the day or where to work.

My doctoral dissertation in 1993[1] researched work/family benefits in a large insurance company. The book chapter I wrote in 1995[2] about the promise and the pitfalls, discussed my eldercare research results of the dissertation on how an organization's good intentions in creating work/life policies came with harsh consequences if you took them.

When I researched women who worked in technology in 2005[3], I thought I would find equitable work/life distribution. The women, however, reported that their partners did help when asked, however, the same issues remained as twenty years before. Women were still primarily responsible for care.

I suggest that the next asymmetric leap arose from the cataclysmic event of the 2020 pandemic. Suddenly, vast networks of workplaces and schools shut down in the US. Precautions against catching the deadly COVID-19 virus precluded coming together in the workplace. Within weeks, organizations pivoted from a rigid case-by-case basis for teleworking and organized people other than front-line first responders, to work remotely with built-in flexibility of time.

We got through the pandemic, yet it changed us. People began to value their relationships and loved ones more. People appreciated getting back to school, and socializing and didn't take life for granted. Millennials and Zoomers had already awakened to live in a way that saw work as a part of the whole and not the whole itself.

What changed is that leaders and organizations recognized this too, because they also lived through the pandemic experience. CEOs had an epiphany that empathy and kindness were okay in the workplace. When leaders trusted employees, allowed for flexibility, and showed empathy with kindness, the workforce responded with greater trust and productivity than before.

Living life and family as primary, and working as a *component* of life, is my preference. It turns out that Millennials and Zoomers were assertive in letting companies know that work is important, but living a *life that works* for them is primary. Companies got the message when recruits would turn down positions because of work/life issues. While the wheels of time and culture tend to grind slowly, the pandemic accelerated the organizational culture's acceptance of flexibility and a hybrid workforce as mainstream. This opportune moment for individual and organizational change isn't lost on me.

I recognize it as a time for the adaptive leader to step forward. Adaptability in life and work is true for individuals and for leaders. It is the new name of competitive advantage. Adaptability is consistently in the top ten most important skills for leaders today. It also happens to be, I suggest one of the most desirable skills for men and women in solving the challenges in both work and life.

Turning Work/life Balance on its Head

Work/life balance or equity are meaningless terms for me. Life and work, yes, are interdependent. Yet, there are a host of other factors that are left out in this two-factor equation. There's a more holistic approach we can take. Consider that the system, the context, and even the day-to-day events in the uncertain world we live in, are constantly evolving. Change is the only constant. An adaptive approach is a robust approach that no rules for the road or a list can match in a rapidly escalating world of uncertainty. The unknowable events of 9/11, COVID-19, and long-simmering wars of increased violence are capable of world devastation with the press of a button. This led me to flip work/life balance on its head, calling it simply: *Living a Life That Works.* This at least captures a framework for thinking that life, rather than work, is primary. The outcome is a life lived well with your loved ones within your community, in your way.

Flashing back to my narrative, I recognize that adaptability has been my go-to strategy throughout my *life that works* journey. I have also been integrating research regarding *adaptability* into my *life that works* coaching with global executives. They benefit from a workable framework for reaching their full potential in their lives and work. These adaptive strategies and applications emerged from my experience and the thousands of executives I have coached.

7 ADAPTIVE SECRETS, STRATEGIES AND APPLICATIONS

The seven adaptive secrets and strategies below are an easy-to-follow framework that includes exercises designed for practice in the workplace or your own life.

SECRET ONE:

Work/life balance is a myth. Balance is a social construct no longer useful in today's world of dynamic change. The good news about social construction is that you can always create a new one.

STRATEGY …

Surrender the concept of work and home balance as the holy grail. Shift your mindset to living an adaptive life, while loosening the demand for a certain outcome. Your input involves devoting your specific skillset to or learning new skills for the task or project. When you shift your mindset from work and life as two competing opposites and include a range of different areas in your life in the picture, you'll notice there is a choice in dialing up or down the various variables. With this outlook, it becomes easier to ask for the help you need in supporting the whole system, as these people are an integral part of that system! You'll begin to recognize as organic, the choice to involve your partner, family, and friends to support you in difficult times and not go it alone.

APPLICATION …

This simple exercise will bring the strategy to life. Draw a circle. Create a spoke for each area beyond life and career that is important for you. Audit how well you think you are doing in these areas using a 1-10 rating system (10 being the highest). For example, it could be:

Taking care of your health 7

Nurturing and sustaining friendships 5

Practicing good nutrition 8

Maintaining good sleep habits 6

Engaging with your spirituality 4

Now that you have completed your assessment, what are your priorities, where are your gaps? Consider what you want to do more or less of. Where are the surprises? What actions do you want to take?

SECRET TWO

Let go of the need for perfection. Perfection will never get you the attention, recognition, or approval you may unconsciously seek. You cannot be everything to all people at the same time. Let go of always saying yes to others and putting yourself last. You don't have to be the lone ranger hero. Get your voice heard and ask for help.

STRATEGY ...

Unlearning is a meta skill according to Brassey and De Samet.[4] It is about being comfortable with not knowing. Let go of what used to work for you, like everything had to be perfect. Replace it with new learning skills like asking for help. Consider replacing wanting perfection with things being good enough and you being good enough. Have fun with these strategies. My clients tell me they use them as "mantras" and pull them out when needed.

APPLICATION ...

1. When I perseverate, I sing or hum the line from Kenny Rodger's song: "Know when to hold them, and when to fold them, and when to let go."

2. Let it go. It's good enough

3. I don't have to do this. I am good enough. I am worthy.

SECRET THREE

Get in touch with your life and work values, otherwise, people will be more than happy to define them for you. Figure out how you want to live your life and what you want out of work and career. Then live a life and find work that is aligned with your values.

STRATEGY ...

Make certain that your values for life and work are in sync. When the two are not at odds research indicates that your inoculation against stress is far greater.

APPLICATION ...

Have a conversation with your partner and discuss and clarify your values. Once crystallized, allow them to become your north star. Internalizing this clear list of values will become your adaptive advantage because you have a foundation on which to make decisions.

SECRET FOUR

Train your brain to shift from a fixed mindset to a growth mindset.

STRATEGY ...

Shifting from "my way or the highway" or black-and-white thinking of a fixed mindset is key to adaptive leadership and leading a fulfilling life. This is true at the individual, team, or organizational level. When a leader -- and we are all leaders of one sort or another – orients herself to a growth mindset it means she has learned how to swivel his brain for a 360 perspective and takes in all angles. Only then does he tackle an issue, or solve any challenge, from lifework dilemmas to market volatility. We see possibilities that were not there before because, now taking in the broadest view, we intentionally look for them, instead of accepting the narrow view.

APPLICATION ...

Prepare yourself ahead of time for the next life or work challenge that arises. Take a step back and consider looking at the problem as one would through a prism of many colors. Then think of many possibilities to resolve the challenge to maximize the interest of stakeholders. (Stakeholders can mean the board and customers, or you and your partner or children.) Practice this until the growth mindset becomes your default way of thinking.

SECRET FIVE

Develop and flex your adaptability muscle by learning Mental Fitness or Mental Flexibility. The adaptability muscle is about flexing forward, while resilience is bouncing back and mental flexibility is exchanging one idea for another or seeing different possibilities.

STRATEGY ...

The strategy here is learning, when deciding, to hold two opposing views at the same time. Traditionally we think of decisions or conflicts as a win-lose situation. However, many times there are alternatives we don't see because we don't look for them in the right places. Often in a conflict what appears intractable may not be. Two people may fight over an orange but come to find out that one needs the rind and the other wants the juice. Deals can be made. Or the conflict may only exist on a position level, and an interest level, and the conflict dissolves.

APPLICATION ...

When you and your partner or colleague have a life or work conflict, check in with your head/heart/gut about what the real challenge is. Are you angry about something else, but are making it about this other issue? Do you know what you truly need rather than want? Bring an adaptive and growth mindset to the issue, sit side by side, and look at the problem together. Watch the dynamic shift. Start discussing where you both agree. Often people don't realize how much they agree on. Build on a base of agreement and flex your adaptability muscle. You are likely to see solutions that weren't in your purview before.

SECRET FIVE

Embrace continuous *unlearning and learning*. The knowledge we gain can quickly outdate what came before. We don't use fax machines, telephone booths, or rotary phones. Our minds let go of the know-how in using the old to learn something else that's better.

If only we could unlearn the entrenched culture of bias and live one of inclusion and solidarity in our work culture.

STRATEGY ...

Continuous learning is a critical part of strategy for most organizations. Keeping up with rapid technological, social, and workplace cultural practices has become the responsibility of everyone in the organization if they want to stay valuable.

APPLICATION ...

Consider how you like to learn. Books and webinars may not be your speed. Maybe AR and VR are better suited for you. Tap into the modality that is right for you and choose one thing you can start on right away: one webinar, one article, or a short book -- and follow the yellow brick road of knowledge.

SECRET SIX

Communicate often. Listen to others until you adapt to understanding people from their point of view. This is instead of listening to the other with the agenda and figuring out how to win them over to your point of view.

STRATEGY ...

When you listen fully and are present in the moment with another to the extent that the other person feels heard, you build trust. Trust is the cornerstone of influence. Adapting your listening style to be in tune with the other is a strategy that will make solving life/work dilemmas, customer problems, or inter-team challenges easier because trust has been built.

APPLICATION ...

Take a hot-button topic for you and a partner or colleague. Decide who will start, and have the other person listen quietly for five minutes. The listener responds with mirroring "I understand you are discussing XYZ, and you would like to know ABC. Is that accurate?" The first step is to check for accuracy in your understanding of assumptions. Very often we make assumptions that the meaning we attribute is the same as what the meaning is for the other person. So many issues come down to mistakenly getting the meaning behind the assumptions wrong.

SECRET SEVEN

Emotional regulation and resilience are related to adaptability, yet they are different enough to deserve a separate category. Managing one's emotions and staying calm during a crisis, whether in life or the workplace, is an important component of the adaptive leader. Being emotionally and mentally resilient means coping with stress *and bouncing back*, which are invaluable skills. The adaptability muscle adds one key element. The resilient person picks herself up and bounces back to face the reality of the situation as it presents itself. The adaptive leader, goes beyond coping with knotty issues, adding value and changing the situation for the better.

STRATEGY ...

Emotional regulation requires intentional awareness of your triggers and the capacity to stop an overblown response before it happens. Easy to say; not so easy to do.

APPLICATION ...

Consider your likely triggers before going into your next meeting. Give some thought to how you want to choose to respond instead of slipping into your typical knee-jerk response or your usual dysregulated outburst. Once you have identified your triggers, select a strategy for reminding yourself to pause. (example: there's that trigger again; breathe in one or two nose breaths, exhale). That one moment is all you need to turn off the amygdala switch and flip on the executive function to help you calmly respond.

EPILOGUE

The 7 Secrets and Strategies for Living a Life That Works is a simple framework for living to your full potential in your life and career. Review the strategies and practice the applications. See what resonates with you, try them out, and build on small successes. A habit takes only 30 days to take hold.

For Leaders

You can flex the adaptability muscle for yourself, your teams, and your organization. Remember that Millennials and Zoomers have come to insist on these features for themselves and their organizations. The volatile market and world we live in demand these features as well.

For Those of Us Who Want to Live a Life that Works

We have the choice to co-create the world we live in, by living our values. We have the responsibility to speak up so that organizations take responsibility for developing a kinder more compassionate workplace that creates adaptive leaders and policies to live our best selves. Your voice matters. Mindy is happy to continue the conversation and support you and your organization in living a *life that works*.

***

To contact Dr. Mindy:

mgewirtz@collaborativenetworks.net

http://www.collaborativenetworks.net

http://www.linkedin.com/in/collaborativenetworks

http://www.21conversationsecrets

References

1. Gewirtz, Mindy, The Promise and the Premise of Eldercare, published 1993.
2. Gewirtz, Mindy "The Promise and the Practice of Eldercare Initiatives in the Corporate Culture" in *Human Dilemmas in the Workplace* Editor Abe Korman, Guilford Press (1994).
3. Gewirtz Mindy and Lindsay, Ann, *Women in the New Economy*, Research Whitepaper, GLS Consulting, 2005.
4. Brassey Jacqueline and DeSemet, Aaron. Future Proof: Solving the Adaptability Paradox for the Long Term, in Mckinsey Newsletter, July 25, 2020.

Afterword

Life and business are always a series of transitions... people, places, and things that shape who we are as individuals. Often, you never know that the next catalyst for improving your business and life is around the corner, in the next person you meet, next mentor you hire or the next book you read.

Jim Britt has spent over four decades influencing individuals and entrepreneurs with strategies to grow their business, developing the right mindset and mental toughness to thrive in today's business environment and to live a better life overall. Allowing all you have read in this book to create a new you, to reinvent yourself and your business model if required, because every business and life level requires a different you. It is your journey to craft.

Cracking the Rich Code is a series that offers much more than a book. It is a community of like-minded influencers from around the world. A global movement. Each chapter is like opening a surprise gift, that just may contain the one idea that changes everything for you. Watch for future releases and add them to your collection.

The work of Jim Britt has filled seminar rooms to maximum capacity and created a worldwide demand. If you get the opportunity to attend one of his live events, jump at the chance. You'll be glad you did.

Become a coauthor: If you are a coach, speaker, consultant of entrepreneur and would like to get the details about becoming a coauthor in the next Cracking the Rich Code book in the series, contact Jim britt at: support@jimbritt.com

STRUGGLING WITH MONEY ISSUES?

Check out Jim's latest program "Cracking the Rich Code" which focuses on the subconscious programs influencing one's financial success, that keeps most living a life of mediocrity. This powerful four-month program is designed to change one's relationship with money and reset your money programming to that of the wealthy. More details at: www.CrackingTheRichCode.com

To Schedule Jim Britt as a featured speaker at your next convention or special event, online or live, email: support@jimbritt.com

Master each moment as they become hours that become days.

Make it a great life!

Your legacy awaits!

STAY IN TOUCH

www.JimBritt.com

www.JimBrittCoaching.com

www.CrackingTheRichCode.com

www.PowerOfLettingGo.com for 2 FREE audios

www.JimBrittAcademy.com

www.ingramcontent.com/pod-product-compliance
Lightning Source LLC
LaVergne TN
LVHW021805060526
838201LV00058B/3247